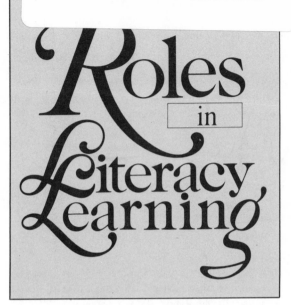

Roles in
Literacy
Learning

A New Perspective

Edited by

Duane R. Tovey
James E. Kerber
The Ohio State U.

D1118456

International Reading Association
800 Barksdale Road   Newark, DE 19714

INTERNATIONAL READING ASSOCIATION

OFFICERS
1985-1986

Copyright 1986 by the
International Reading Association, Inc.

Library of Congress Cataloging in Publication Data
Main entry under title:

Roles in literacy learning.

 Bibliography: p.
 1. Reading—Addresses, essays, lectures. 2. Reading—Parent
involvement—Addresses, essays, lectures. 3. Children—Books and
reading—Addresses, essays, lectures. I. Tovey, Duane R. II. Kerber,
James E.
LB1050.R58 1986   372.4   85-17691
ISBN 0-87207-962-7

Contents

Foreword   *vi*

Introduction   *vii*

Part One   Role of the Parents

Overview of the Role   1

Learning to Read: It Starts in the Home   *David B. Doake*   2

Let's Read Another One   *Diane L. Chapman*   10

Literacy Environment in the Home and Community
Yetta M. Goodman and *Myna M. Haussler*   26

Part Two   Role of the Teacher

Overview of the Role   33

Teaching and Language Centered Programs   *MaryAnne Hall*   34

Guiding a Natural Process   *Don Holdaway*   42

Nourishing and Sustaining Reading   *Margaret Meek Spencer*   52

Part Three   Role of the Child

Overview of the Role   65

Apprenticeship in the Art of Literacy   *Anne D. Forester*   66

Children's Quest for Literacy   *John McInnes*   73

Children Write to Read and Read to Write   *Diane E. DeFord*   79

Part Four   Role of the Administrator

Overview of the Role   95

Emergence of an Administrator   *Marilyn D. Reed*   96

Removing the "We-They" Syndrome   *G. William Stratton*   105

Cultivating Teacher Power   *Moira G. McKenzie*   113

Part Five   Role of the Researcher

Overview of the Role   133

Theory, Practice, and Research in Literacy Learning
Robert Emans   135

Reading Research at the One Century Mark
Edmund H. Henderson   145

The Researcher, Whole Language, and Reading
William D. Page   156

A Postscript   167
References   170

The International Reading Association attempts, through its publications, to provide a forum for a wide spectrum of opinions on reading. This policy permits divergent viewpoints without assuming the endorsement of the Association.

Contributors

Diane L. Chapman
Ohio State University
Columbus, Ohio

Diane E. DeFord
Ohio State University
Columbus, Ohio

David D. Doake
Acadia University
Wolfville, Nova Scotia

Robert Emans
University of South Dakota
Vermillion, South Dakota

Anne D. Forester
Camosun College
Victoria, British Columbia

Yetta M. Goodman
University of Arizona
Tucson, Arizona

MaryAnne Hall
Georgia State University
Atlanta, Georgia

Myna Haussler
University of Arizona
Tucson, Arizona

Edmund H. Henderson
University of Virginia
Charlottesville, Virginia

Don Holdaway
Watertown, Massachusetts

James E. Kerber
Ohio State University
Columbus, Ohio

John McInnes
Ontario Institute for Studies in Education
Toronto, Ontario

Moira McKenzie
Peddington, Middlesex
United Kingdom

William D. Page
University of Connecticut
Storrs, Connecticut

Marilyn D. Reed
Barrington Elementary School
Columbus, Ohio

Margaret Meek Spencer
University of London
London, England

G. William Stratton
Etobicoke Board of Education
Etobicoke, Ontario

Duane R. Tovey
Ohio State University
Columbus, Ohio

This book is dedicated to the memory of William D. Page who contributed greatly to the cause of linking language research and students' linguistic competence to the reading task.

Foreword

All the world's a stage,
And all the men and women merely players.
They have their exits and their entrances;
And one man in his time plays many parts,...

(Shakespeare, *As You Like It*)

So it is with literacy learning; many people have a role to play. The roles shift, but each one is crucial in its own time. David Doake shows what the first role is like for the parents of the mewling infant; the roles of others build on what the parents have done as the child grows.

Literate people hand down a kind of magic when they teach a child to read and write. And what a joyful process it is when every player plays a role to its fullest.

The growing body of research on how children become literate naturally is causing us to change many of the old ways we taught reading and writing. We know that knowledge does not exist outside a learner; it is constructed and actively discovered by the learner. Children make sense of new learning, including reading and writing, when they relate it to what they already know. The authors in this volume respect the child as a learner and show how the roles of parent, teacher, administrator, and researcher interact as the child becomes literate.

There is a great deal of discussion in this volume about an environment conducive to literacy learning. We know the kind of environment it takes to help children become literate; we know what people need to do to provide that enriching environment. The sections on guiding a natural process stress the collaborative role between teachers and children. Sections on nourishing and sustaining literate behavior show that the child is in the lead. The sections on apprenticeships and children's quest for literacy indicate a new relationship between beginners and those of us who practice the craft of literacy well. There is also a new relationship defined for the administrator, researcher, and teacher as they are linked together with the literacy learner.

The International Reading Association has a responsibility to keep its members abreast of the latest findings of research on reading and writing. The Association is also responsible for helping members translate that research into effective teaching practices. By publishing this collection of articles, IRA is fulfilling both of these responsibilities in an admirable way.

Bernice E. Cullinan
New York University

Introduction

One of the first books published in the United States regarding reading instruction was written by Edmund Burke Huey in 1908 (*137*). Surprisingly, many of Huey's ideas are in keeping with recent language research findings. His emphasis on meaning concurred with more recent psycholinguistic findings when he stated:

> The child should never be permitted to read for the sake of reading, as a formal process or end in itself. The reading should always be for the intrinsic interest or value of what is read, reading never being done or thought of as "an exercise." Word pronouncing will therefore always be secondary to getting whole sentence-meanings, and this from the very first.

Meaning was also viewed as primary in *The Horace Mann Readers* published in 1912:

> "Let Thought Lead." The principle here involved is nothing less than the recognition of the truth that, as children are essentially thinking beings, we must in dealing with them "et thought lead." In teaching children to read there is no principle of more fundamental or more practical importance than this. For whatever is learned under the impulse of the thought is more easily learned and more vitally remembered than anything learned by mere repetition.

In a recent book dealing with the history of reading and writing instruction, Robinson (*187*) provided even more evidence that meaning centered reading instruction was in vogue during the first quarter of this century (1910-1925):

> A true innovation...emerged—emphasis on silent reading. The rather rapid change from stress on oral reading to the vigorous teaching of silent reading was probably related to several factors. There were increasing demands placed on reading for meaning, instead of on oral exercise, in order to meet the varied needs of society.

The 1920s, however, saw the advent of educational measurement, testing, and research, influencing not only research, which tended to be restricted to topics and tasks which could be measured objectively, but teaching and curriculum decisions as well. Continued attempts at formalizing teaching practices and methods during the 1930s and 1940s were influenced not only by objectivism and attempts to quantify, but were also greatly dependent on commonsense ideas of how reading works and how it should be taught. Traditionally, initial instruction has started with learning the names of the letters of the alphabet and their respective sounds, eventually emphasizing the meaning such symbols represent. This fragmented view of reading—going from the parts to the whole—fit well with the quantitative orientation of the experimentalists. The "bits and pieces" of language also complemented both the format and content of programmatic materials such as worksheets, workbooks, and teacher manuals which contained numerous exercises and drills. Consequently, during the past 50 years, the teaching of reading has been greatly influenced by prescribed programs which frequently stressed the objective/mechanical aspects of reading rather than reading as a meaning centered process.

During the past two decades, though, since the publication of Noam Chomsky's *Syntactic Structures* in 1957 (*42*) and the advent of transformational grammar, researchers have devoted a great deal of time and energy to language acquisition studies and language learning in general. During the 1960s, Goodman (*96*) borrowed from this language-learning-research methodology and adapted it to his qualitative miscue research. These and other language related reading studies suggest that reading is not a simple compilation of skills to be "poured" into children's minds, but "a skill" of processing whole language which is a much more complex task than previously thought. Hence, learning to read can more appropriately be thought of as implicit language learning, rather than the conscious learning of a plethora of "reading skills." Fortunately, during this period, a greater understanding and appreciation of children's language processing abilities have also emerged, which seem to suggest that children can learn to read quite naturally if instructional procedures are in keeping with their linguistic competencies and abilities.

How, then, can instructional procedures be altered to capitalize on children's language processing abilities? What linguistic abilities and competencies do children bring with them to the reading task? What role should parents play in literacy learning? How can administrators help teachers implement reading programs in keeping with current language learning research? Do researchers have useful information for classroom teachers, or are their findings too impractical?

In this book we consider questions such as these in light of the new knowledge that linguists, psycholinguists, and reading researchers have produced during the past 20 years. There appears to be a real need for redefining and better understanding the roles parents, teachers, administrators, and researchers play in helping children fulfill their role of actively learning to process written language. If children's incomparable language abilities are to be linked appropriately with the overwhelmingly complex task of learning to read, those assisting must understand the reading process and how language is learned.

DRT

JEK

Part One   Role of the Parents

Overview of the Role

Traditionally, parents and other family members have been reluctant to help their preschoolers read for fear of creating problems for them when they enter school. These feelings seem to be based on three assumptions: 1) Teachers have access to esoteric and specialized knowledge about "the right way" to teach reading; 2) reading programs are designed by experts and therefore are theoretically sound; and 3) parents shouldn't meddle.

On the other hand, early reader studies have consistently indicated the importance of parents reading to their children, encouraging their initial reading efforts, and answering their questions as they become more and more involved in deciphering the meaning of print they see on television, billboards, product labels, and other materials. When reading is viewed as implicit language learning rather than the conscious learning of "skills," the parents' role becomes critically important and similar to the role played during their children's aural-oral language learning.

In "Learning to Read: It Starts in the Home," Doake demonstrates the inner drive of young children for becoming readers even before their first birthday. He suggests that children have the right to be read to from the day of birth. In "Let's Read Another One," Chapman expands Doake's contribution by suggesting specific objectives for parents to achieve informally in book sharing sessions with their children. "Literacy Environment in the Home and Community," ends the first section of this book with Goodman and Haussler extending their preschool literacy experiences from the home into the community. They also provide specific suggestions for promoting increased cooperation between the home and school in achieving improved literacy learning.

Learning to Read: It Starts in the Home

David B. Doake

For many years learning to read has been thought of as a secondary or derived language learning task, dependent upon some predetermined level of competence in oral language. In this view, children must learn to talk before they can begin to learn to read. While parents have been actively encouraged to facilitate the oral language development of their children in naturalistic ways, they have been actively discouraged, by teachers in particular, from promoting the reading development of their children.

Apart from exhorting parents to read to their children to assist in the generalized growth of an interest in books and in reading, teachers have traditionally guarded the domain of providing reading instruction for children upon their entry to school. This "guardianship" has been exerted and maintained through a belief that learning to read is a complex process that has to be taught to children after they are five or six years old and that this teaching should occur via the presentation of an extensive series of carefully sequenced skills. The control of the learning to read process then, some teachers claim, has to be left in their hands since only they possess a comprehensive knowledge of this sequence of skills and how to teach them. Only they have available appropriate materials to provide the children with the necessary practice to develop mastery over the skills.

Some evidence now demonstrates that this view of learning to read is in serious error. Instead, we should view learning to read as an outcome of the child's natural experiences with written language in the home which the school then extends and develops. Teachers would do well to examine in some detail the characteristics of homes which produce children who either learn to read before they go to school or whose learning proceeds with ease after they enter school, regardless of the nature of the instruction they receive.

The results of a variety of studies have brought a different view of how young children can and do go about the process of learning to read when given the opportunity to do so. Case histories of early readers, for example, clearly demonstrate that young children can learn to read before they go to school, frequently without instruction and occasionally without their parents being aware that they have learned to read (*43, 66, 86, 178*). The outstanding feature which seemed to contribute most to these children's early reading development was that they came from print oriented homes and had been read to extensively from a very early age. Because these studies of early readers were retrospective in nature, they could not indicate how this wealth of experience with books and reading contributed to reading development, but observational studies conducted in the homes of preschool children have been able to do so with an increasing degree of specificity (*20, 49, 58, 130, 225*). Finally, two studies, one by Soderbergh (*213*) with severely deaf preschoolers who learned to read and write without having access to oral language, the other by Steinberg and Steinberg (*218*) who taught their son, Kimio, to read before he could talk, demonstrated that oral language acquisition was not an essential precondition for written language learning.

Results of these and similar studies have made obvious the necessity of viewing the process of learning to read quite differently. We must see reading as a primary language learning activity, the learning of which can and should begin in the same way and at the same time as oral language. Just as there is no such thing as a period of "talking readiness," there is no period of "reading readiness." Children who grow up in book oriented homes begin to learn to read when they are held in their parents' arms and are read their first nursery rhyme, story, or jingle.

By frequently sharing in the repeated reading of favorite stories, children will demonstrate that they not only enjoy the experience tremendously, but that they want to participate actively as well. As their oral language develops, so does their ability to reproduce their favorite stories in readinglike ways. Provided that their approximating and experimental efforts to retrieve the language of their books are met with the same noncorrective, strongly supportive response that meets their attempts to produce meaningful oral language, they will almost certainly continue to direct their energies intuitively toward gaining independent access to their favorite stories. Just as with oral language learning, adults can give children the opportunity to direct, regulate and monitor their own learning-to-read strategies and processes. And just as learning oral language is made possible through the countless hours of joyful interaction which occurs between parent and child, so too does learning to read originate in the same type of interaction which occurs when loving parents spend time with their children and their books.

Establishing an Inner Drive to Want to Learn to Read

Observational studies conducted in the book oriented homes of preschool children have provided an increasingly clear understanding of the crucial role that reading to and with children plays in their reading development. When reading experiences begin at birth like oral language does, extremely powerful and positive attitudes toward books and reading are established. Playing with books becomes a preferred activity, book handling knowledge is developed, and attention spans when listening to familiar stories grow to be virtually inexhaustible. The warm, human sharing which occurs when books, parents, and children come together becomes permanently associated with reading and creates an inner drive for gaining personal control over this experience.

It is said that a picture is worth a thousand words. The series of photographs at the end of this chapter demonstrates clearly how quickly very young children can become "hooked on books." They were taken at intervals over the period of the first year of this child's (Raja) life.

Raja was read to on the day he was born and on virtually every day following. Some of the stories that were read to him on a regular basis during the first few months of his life were Mercer Meyer's *Just For You*; Bill Martin's *Brown Bear, Brown Bear What Do You See?*; and Ethel and Leonard Kessler's *Do Baby Bears Sit in Chairs?* These and other stories were pleasant to read and easy to listen to, repetitive, rhyming, and flowing and therefore highly predictable (*190*).

For the first two months, Raja paid little obvious attention to the books but would simply lie passively in the reader's arms looking around the room, at the reader's face, and occasionally at the book. At 2 months, 3 days, however, as he was lying in his rocker and beginning to cry, *Just for You* was held in front of him (as in the photograph) and read. He stopped crying immediately, looked at the pages of the book, and never took his eyes off them until the story was finished. Two more familiar stories were then read to him and he listened with the same continuous attending behavior. From that time on, he would sit and listen and look with a high degree of attention as familiar stories were read and reread. His visual inspection of the pages was both careful and comprehensive.

By 2 months, 3 weeks he had begun to touch the pages of his books. He could be sitting on a parent's knees quietly and passively, but would become active and animated as soon as a familiar book was read to him. The avidness of his attending behavior was very closely related to his degree of familiarity with the story. For example, between 3 and 4 months, he was being read a series of familiar stories when a new story was read to him. He immediately became restless and distracted; but when, after a few pages, the reader turned to a familiar one, his avid attention returned. This pattern was repeated three times, each time with different stories, with the same result. New stories usually had to be introduced gradually, with a few pages being read at each sitting.

Although his familiarity with the books' illustrations may have been partially responsible for his different reactions to familiar and unfamiliar stories, Raja was identifying with the sound of the language. For example, a familiar story recited without the book could consistently act as a pacifier, no matter how disturbed he was. Even a piercing scream produced by a vaccination shot was stilled by his father reciting "Brown Bear, Brown Bear, What do you see?" With the needle still in his arm, Raja started to laugh. Such is the power of the joyful associations he developed with the language of his repeatedly read stories.

By 5 months, Raja had an attention span of at least 40 minutes as his repertoire of 15 familiar stories was read to him, three of which were in Arabic. By 6 months, he was responding with smiles and excited stretching to particular words (Meow; Boom; No-oooo!) when the reader emphasized them. By 8 months, he emitted a contented sigh or smiled up at the reader when the last page was turned and read. He also began reacting to certain illustrations or parts of illustrations by pointing to them, or as in one case, by pulling the page up to his mouth, demonstrating great enjoyment as he did so.

By 9 months, Raja's attention span for listening to familiar stories had increased to at least 75 minutes, and he now had a library of 22 books. He started to turn the pages as the stories were read to him and to flatten them down delicately. By around 10 months, he had become aware that the pages of the English stories were turned in a direction opposite from the pages of the Arabic stories. He would turn them either by the reader's request or by seemingly recognizing that the page was finished from the sound of the reader's voice.

He also began to reach over and deliberately close an unfamiliar book after only a few pages, although he would demonstrate immediate interest in some new books and allow them to be read right through. *Over in the Meadow* by John Langstaff was one such book. During the first reading, he laughed at repetitive lines, such as " 'Dig,' said the mother. 'I dig,' said the one. So he dug and was glad in the sand in the sun." His laughter grew more and more hilarious as the story continued, the book immediately becoming a favorite. His attention span by this stage seemed virtually inexhaustible and was controlled only by his parent's available time.

During Raja's eleventh month, he started to identify some of his favorite books by name when asked to bring one to a parent. He could be drawn from almost any other activity simply by someone beginning to read one of his familiar stories. He began spending long periods of time (up to 45 minutes on occasions) in independent play with his books, gaining mastery over opening them and turning their pages, laughing at certain pages. His library of familiar stories had grown to 32. In addition to listening to his parents read to him, he would also listen attentively to audiotaped versions of stories read by Bill Martin, Jr., and other such performers. As well as being extremely active during his waking hours, Raja obviously found great pleasure in spending many quieter hours with his books which, by now, had become an integral part of his life.

Throughout the first year of his life, Raja was read to approximately 45 minutes to an hour each day. On some days he was not read to at all, but on others for one or possibly two hours. Both his mother and father read to him, the mother reading probably twice as much as the father. His mother also read to him in Arabic. The aim of providing Raja with this regular experience with books from birth was not to try and make him into an early reader but simply to share an activity which both parents enjoyed immensely. Within two months, Raja also demonstrated his enjoyment of the experience, and evidence of this grew rapidly as the year progressed.

When the child, a parent, and a book came together something almost magical happened. The inner need to develop ways of gaining independent access to his books so that he could retrieve these moments of magic and pleasure for himself was already evident in Raja's behavior by the end of his first year.

Conclusion

The parents' responsibility for providing a print oriented environment for their children from as early in their lives as possible is obvious. To deny children this experience is similar to and as serious as denying them the opportunity of hearing oral language. All children have the right to be read to! All children have the right to the irreplaceable pleasure of being held in their parents' arms and hearing loved stories again and again. All children have the right to manage the process of learning to read for themselves from the basis of an inner drive created by the countless hours in the company of their books and a loved parent. And if the home does not provide children with these experiences and opportunities, then the school must.

If all parents accepted their responsibility of reading regularly to and with their children, there would be little worry about television dominating the living rooms of the nation and the lives and minds of our children. Our children would become "hooked on books" rather than "hooked on the box." The number of children who fail to make books and reading an integral part of their lives would be reduced dramatically. In addition, schools must abandon teacher-oriented and teacher-dominated methods of reading instruction and incorporate the naturalistic methods and memorable books used so successfully by parents who read regularly to their children.

Raja gets hooked on books...a first year chronology

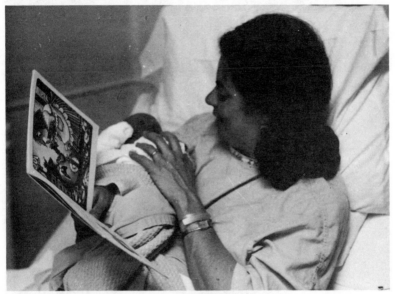

Reading begins (6 hours old)

What's all this about? (2 months, 3 days)

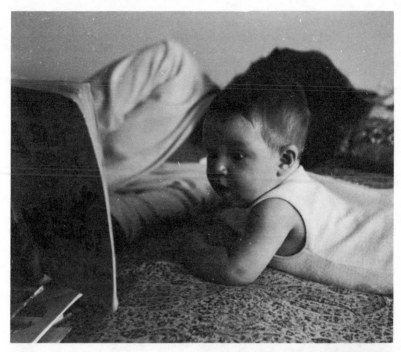

That looks interesting!
(4 months)

I'm enjoying this story!
(5 months)

Warm, human sharing (6 months)

How do these pages work? (9 months)

I'm a reader! (10 months)

Let's Read Another One

Diane L. Chapman

Jeff, four and a half years old, is enjoying Carle's *The Very Hungry Caterpillar* with his mother. Reading it aloud for the second time, Jeff's mother changes the text.

Jeff's Mother	Jeff
"On Monday he ate through one apple, but he was still hungry. On Tuesday he ate through Jeffrey and he was still hungry."*	
	What did it say?
It said, "On Tuesday he ate through Jeffrey."	
	No!
"On Tuesday he ate through two pears, but he was still hungry."	
	Yeah!

Is Jeff a reader? No, not in the conventional sense. He does not yet independently gain meaning from print. But Jeff knows what to expect—and what *not* to expect—from book text. He knows that the text says things. When someone reads, he explains, "They just read the words, what they say."

At four and a half, Jeff handles books easily. On his own with a stack of picture books, he looks at each one methodically. Page by page, left to right, front to back, he searches the pictures for meaning. When his mother is present, he taps her ability as a reader to gain access to the meaning in the text. "What does it say?" he asks, pointing to the title of a new

---

*Note: Quotation marks indicate words read directly from the book being shared. Words not in quotation marks are utterances made by the parent or the child.

book. "Let's read it again!" he demands as they come to the end of a well liked story. Is Jeff a reader? Not really. Is he a nonreader? Definitely not! Does Jeff think of himself as a reader? Yes and no. While his mother was being interviewed about Jeff's early experiences with books, he interrupted with: "Mommy, you forgot to tell her I read a book one day all by myself, and you didn't help me!" But later he is not so sure:

Jeff's Mother	*Jeff*
	This is the beginning and this is the end.
How can you tell?	'Cause I read it over there.
Oh, did you read it?	No, I just looked at the pictures.

Jeff knows that meaning resides in the text as well as in the pictures. He asks for that meaning to be supplied. Even though when his mother reads to him, his attention is not completely focused on the text, his curiosity about the text propels him toward becoming a more competent reader.

Learning to read is a gradual process that begins early in the child's life, not a sudden happening that comes about when the child enters school. The roots of literacy are anchored within the social network of the family.

When does an American child begin to learn to read? When he watches his mother prepare his food from a can or carton covered with reading material? When he first pays attention to television? When he responds to his mother's 'don't touch'? When he says his first word? When he encounters his first book? (*4*, p. 97)

Emergent reading is a term used to describe the first stage in children's growth toward literacy. As parents share books and stories with children during the preschool years, children acquire a sense of directionality, learning to move through a book as the conventions of written language in their culture require: left to right, top to bottom, front to back for the American child. Children soon begin to attend to print, which eventually enables them to retell a story that at first is page matched and later line and word matched to the text. They also develop an ear for book language, so that they begin to "talk like a book" when they retell stories (*44*).

How does this remarkable growth occur during the preschool years, before most children receive any formal instruction in reading? Meek (*162*) posits that children learn to read when they are encouraged to behave like readers. "Learning to read in the early stages, like everything else a child has come to know, is an approximation of adult behavior with a genuine, meaningful function" (p. 24). Holdaway (*130*) describes young children's approximations of reading as "reading-like play." "Almost unintelligible at first, this reading-like play rapidly becomes picture-stimulated, page-matched, and story-complete" (p. 40). In order to begin the development of literacy during the preschool years children need experiences with print and the guidance of adults who can give them access to the meaning that the print represents. Studies of children who learned to read before they entered school in America (*66*) and in Scotland (*43*) reveal that sharing books with interested adults was characteristic of the early readers' preschool experience. Few of the parents had set out to teach their children to read. Rather, they had simply responded to their children's curiosity about books and other printed materials. A number of these parents expressed uneasiness and even guilt about their role in the children's development of literacy. Apparently these parents viewed learning to read as a process requiring expert help from persons with specialized knowledge. However, Meek (*162*) advises parents that "Reading is too important to be left to the experts" (p. 24). She points out that the role of the parent is unlike that of the teacher:

> The parents' role is different; it is to encourage the child to believe that reading is a worthwhile and pleasurable thing to do, that literacy is within his grasp, and to provide the means for his enjoyment and success. (p. 26)

Parents who read in the home give young children their first models of literacy. For many preschoolers, the parent is the only model of what a reader is. When children observe adults reading, they develop understandings about what reading is and why it is done. If they are fortunate enough to have parents who read to them, they can also begin to develop understandings about how it is done. Downing (*62*), building on an earlier work by Reid (*189*), distinguishes between the functional aspects of and the technical concepts and terms about reading as human beings move toward literacy. Children from oral cultures that do not value written language enter school less aware of the communicative function of written language than children from more literate cultures, nor do they exhibit conceptual and linguistic control of the technical features of language such as letter, word, and sound (*63*). Children who see their parents read soon develop functional concepts about reading. Those whose parents share books and other forms of print with them begin learning the technical concepts about reading as well.

To the not-yet-literate child, the parent holds the key to unlocking the meaning represented by the text. "Read me another one!" and "Read it again!" are the child's means for gaining access to print knowledge and meaning. What takes place when parents share books with children? What is it that parents do to facilitate the child's transition to literacy? To address these questions, naturalistic observations were made of 18 parents sharing books with children ages one and a half to four and a half from three cultural groups present in a midsized midwestern city: low socioeconomic status (SES) urban black, low-SES Appalachian white, and mid-SES mainstream white.* Book sharing episodes were videotaped in quiet areas of the children's preschool centers. Although most parents in the study appeared to function in ways related to the age and developmental level of their children, a number of parental behaviors characterized the parent-child interactions observed. During book sharing, parents frequently related events in books to the child's life, used books to expand the child's world, provided the child with information about books and about reading, helped the child get meaning from pictures, helped the child get meaning from text, and encouraged the child to behave like a reader. Each of these parental behaviors is discussed below.

Relating Events in Books to the Child's Life

Parents often relate characters and events in books to people and happenings in the child's own life. Reading with Elisa (three years, ten months), her mother relates events in Burningham's *The Blanket* to experiences in Elisa's life:

Elisa's Mother	*Elisa*
"When I go to bed, I always take my blanket." Do you remember when Patty used to carry around a blanket all the time? She took her blanket to bed.	
	Why?
Well, it was sort of like when you took your baby lamb to bed. Her blanket was real essential to her. "One night I could not find my blanket." He was feeling bad.	
	Sad?

*Note: These observations were made as part of a larger study, "Early Reading Experiences: Developmental and Ecological Perspectives," conducted by Diane L. Chapman and Rosalind L. Williams and funded by The Ohio State University Small Grant Program.

"Mommy looked in the bathroom. Daddy looked in the cupboard." Oh, no! What happened when he opened the door?

They all felled out.

Like our cupboards at home, isn't it?

Uh-huh.

"And I looked under my bed. But we could not find the blanket." Oh, oh! What's he doing?

He's sucking his thumb.

Who do you know who does that?

Erica.

"Then Mommy looked in the washing"—the laundry basket—"and Daddy looked in the car, but I found the blanket under my pillow and went to sleep."

By relating the boy's need for his lost blanket to Elisa's attachment to her baby lamb, Elisa's mother provides her with a link that enables her to understand the story on a deeper level. The satisfaction of Burningham's simple ending can now take on personal meaning for Elisa. Bridging the story to the child's life makes reading a more meaningful experience.

Expanding the Child's World

Parents can sometimes focus on events in stories in order to enlarge the child's world. When Elisa and her mother share Galdone's *The Three Billy Goats Gruff,* her mother tries to determine what Elisa already knows and how her knowledge can be expanded:

Elisa's Mother	*Elisa*
"I've got two horns and four hard hooves. See what you can do." See his horns? See if they show us his horns. They don't show us his hooves, do they?	Uh-huh.
Look at the horns. What's he doing?	He's not...he's walking on the sky.
Oh, they didn't show the sky and the ground here, did they? What's he doing to the troll?	I don't know.

You know what they call it when goats use their horns like that to push on something?

No.

They call that butting. Butting·

Is the troll scared?

Probably. He's probably scared. He looks pretty scared, doesn't he? Sometimes goats do that to each other if they are fighting. They put their heads down like that and they butt with their horns. "So up climbed that mean ugly troll and the Billy Goat Gruff butted him with his horns and he trampled him with his hard hooves." Still don't see his hooves, do we? Look at him! "And he tossed him over the bridge into the rushing river."

Elisa has not yet developed a firm sense of perspective. Confused by the absence of a horizon line in the illustration, she misinterprets the picture as showing that the goat is walking on the sky. Her mother does not try to develop Elisa's sense of perspective beyond her years. Rather, she offers a brief clarification of the picture and goes on to expand another concept — butting — that she thinks Elisa is ready to grasp. She questions Elisa to find out what she already knows and then uses pictures, words, and a demonstration (motioning with her head) to explain the new concept. As a result, Elisa's understanding of the story is enlarged, along with her knowledge about the world.

Sometimes a book alone is an insufficient way to develop a concept. The mother of two and a half year old Teddy recognizes the need for more direct experience when she and Teddy encounter a tunnel in Crews' *Truck*:

Teddy's Mother	*Teddy*
What's that?	
	A car.
That's a city bus.	
	A city bus.
Uh-huh. And it is coming through the tunnel. And the truck is disappearing into the tunnel. Let's see. And here they are coming out. They went clear through the tunnel.	

We've never taken you through one,
have we? We'll have to go through a
tunnel.

Teddy's world does not yet include tunnels, but his mother knows that he
needs a firsthand experience with tunnels to supplement the information
that the book provides.

Young children sometimes understand concepts in one context but
are unable to transfer them to another context. Karah (2 years, 3 months),
for instance, knows what eyebrows are and recognizes them on people and
in pictures. But her own eyebrows, because they are not readily visible to
her, do not exist in her perceptions of things. Karah's mother discovers this
when they share McNaught's *Muppets in My Neighborhood*:

Karah's Mother	*Karah*
Ernie and Bert! Look, they have got hats on. Do you see their hats?	
	Uh-huh.
Those are nice hats! Look at that nose! Do you see his eyebrows? Where are his eyebrows?	
	There?
Very good! Yeah, eyebrows.	
	Eyebrows.
Have you got eyebrows, too?	
	Uh-huh.
I have eyebrows. See my eyebrows. Do you have eyebrows?	
	No.
You don't have eyebrows?	Uh-huh.
Oh. Who is that? (pointing to the next page)	

Karah's mother is satisfied to allow Karah more time to discover what
physical attributes she shares with others. Sensitive to Karah's level of development, she does not try to expand every concept encountered in a
story. Like Elisa's mother choosing not to address spatial perspective,
Karah's mother considers her daughter's level of development in deciding
which concepts to expand and which to ignore.

Providing Information about Books and about Reading

When parents share books with children, they provide them with the input
to develop technical as well as functional concepts about reading. Most

often this information is shared informally, even incidentally, within the context of book sharing. When Timmy (1 year, 7 months) hands his mother a book, she responds, "You've got it upside down. Turn it around. You can't read it like that." From encounters like this, Timmy will learn how to hold books and how to move through them. Nikia (3 years, 11 months) already knows how to handle books, but when she skips over several pages in Bruna's *b is for bear*, her father responds in a way that tells Nikia that every page is important for full meaning:

Nikia's Father	Nikia
And J is for...	Puzzle.
Um...jigsaw puzzle.	
	And M is for—
	(turning over several pages)
Uh-oh! We skipped a couple of pages. K is for...	
	Key.
Yeah. L is for...what's that?	

Mia (one year, 11 months) is just learning how to handle a book. While her grandmother is sharing a book with her, Mia reaches out to help hold the book, covering a part of the text with her hand. Mia's grandmother says, "Let me see the reading. Move your hand. That's it. You want to hold the book? You can hold the book if you'd like to. Oh, good!" While encouraging Mia to hold the book, her grandmother conveys that it is the text, not the pictures, that contains the message.

Knowing that books have a beginning, middle, and ending is another concept learned through book sharing. When Richie (3 years, 6 months) hands his mother a book to read, he turns to the middle of the book first:

Richie's Mother	Richie
	I want that one. Not all these pages.
	Not all these pages. *These* pages.
Okay. I don't really want to start a book in the middle. Can I start at the beginning? (turning back)	

Richie is learning that books are usually read from front to back, but he is also learning what "the beginning" means—a concept that will be useful to him later in formal instruction.

Courtney (2 years, 3 months) learns about the end of a book by echoing her mother:

Courtney's Mother	*Courtney*
The end.	The end.
Can you find another one? Find another book.	

Jeff (4 years, 6 months) knows how books end, and he enjoys signaling the end of a story:

Jeff's Mother	*Jeff*
	Hey, the end!
The end.	Would you read me another one?
Sure will!	

Book sharing provides opportunities to expose children to other information about reading as well. Mia, for example, is introduced to the idea that books are written by people:

Mia's Grandmother	*Mia*
Would you like for me to read this story to you?	Yeah.
Okay. This story is about the blanket. Okay?	Yeah.
Do you know what a blanket is?	(nods)
Okay. Let's first of all look at who it is written by. You don't know him, but that's okay. Let's see...*The Blanket* by John Burningham. Okay?	

Even though Mia is too young to understand the concept of authorship, Mia will probably be exposed to it again and again through her preschool years as books are shared with her.

Children also learn pagination through shared book experiences. Courtney observes her mother use the table of contents to locate a favorite rhyme in Rojankovsky's *The Tall Book of Mother Goose:*

Courtney's Mother	*Courtney*
This is Mother Goose!	Goose.
I wonder if "Ding, Dong, Bell" is in here. Oh, it is! 74.	Where's "Ding, Dong"?
Page 74. "Ding, Dong, Bell!"	

Chapman

Courtney does not understand the table of contents, nor does Mia know what an author is. But they have been introduced to concepts about books that will be presented to them until they become meaningful.

Much information about reading is imparted informally during book sharing. Children do not acquire this information all at once. But over time they develop a host of understandings about reading and about books.

Helping the Child Get Meaning from Pictures

Long before children pay any attention to text, parents need to encourage them to "read" pictures for meaning. Parents' comments and questions directed to their one, two, and three year old children are excellent means for helping children focus on pictures. In the following dialogue Karah's mother helps her look for meaning in the pictures of Burningham's *The Blanket:*

Karah's Mother	*Karah*
It says, "One night I could not find my blanket." Oh, no! "Mommy looked in the bathroom." Do you see her? Is that the bathroom? Yeah? What do you see? What is that, huh? Do you see a brush? Where is the brush?	
	(points)
Right there on the floor, huh? Somebody dropped the brush. "Daddy looked in the cupboard." Look! Everything fell out! What do you see that fell out? Do you see a broom?	
	What that?
That is a tennis racket.	What that?
What *is* that?	A ball.
A ball. What is that? What's that right there? Do you remember what that's called?	

Mother-child interactions during picture book sharing have been characterized as ritualized dialogues (*168*) and routines, which are recurrent, highly structured, and have been shown to support language acquisition (*212*). According to Ninio and Bruner (*168*), maternal speech during picture book reading often consists of four utterance types: attentional vocative ("Look!"), queries ("What's that?"), labels ("That's an X"), and feedback utterances ("Yes, an X" or "No, not X"). Analyzing the interaction between a mother and her child from six months to 18 months, Ninio and Bruner show that these maternal utterances form the basis of a child's conversation, complete with turn-taking nonverbal responses and vocalizations. Conversation involves a mother and her child in a language game that results in much word learning for the child.

In addition to the labeling routine described by Ninio and Bruner, parents use several other dialogue structures while sharing picture books with their children. These routines, all focusing on the interpretation of meaning represented in pictures, appear to vary with the child's level of language development and with the structure of the book being shared. For instance, Ninio and Bruner found that Timmy's mother asks a preponderance of "Where's X?" questions. Questions of this type allow Timmy, who is preverbal (1 year, 7 months), to respond by pointing, thus demonstrating his ability to identify the object for which his mother has provided a label.

Courtney, on the other hand, has far more advanced language abilities at 2 years, 3 months. Her mother asks few "Where's X?" questions. Instead, when they are reading a book filled with pictures of people and things familiar to Courtney (McNaught's *Muppets in My Neighborhood*), she elicits labels from Courtney with questions like "Who's that?".

Courtney's Mother	*Courtney*
Sesame Street. Sit up nice and straight. Who is that?	Big Bird.
Who is that?	Cookie Monster.
Who is that?	Grover.
Who is that?	Big Bird.
That's Big Bird. (turning back to an earlier page)	Big Bird.
Who is that? Is that Bert?	Bert.
That's right.	

When sharing a book filled with less familiar objects such as Bruna's *b is for bear,* Courtney and her mother establish a repetition routine which provides Courtney with a label whenever she needs it. Mother provides labels for the unfamiliar letters and objects, and Courtney responds by echoing both her mother's words and intonations.

Courtney's Mother	Courtney
That's a good one. Sure.	
"b is for bear."	
	For bear.
Yes. B is for bear.	
	B is for bear.
A.	
	A.
Apple.	
	Apple.

Teddy (2 years, 5 months) is in the holophrasic or one word stage of language development. In reading Burningham's *The Blanket,* Teddy's mother establishes a fill-in-the-blank routine that is well matched to Teddy's one word utterances:

Teddy's Mother	Teddy
"When I go to bed, I always take my..."	
	Goggy.
Blanket. Your goggy. "But one night I could not find my blanket." Look at him. He says, "Where's my blanket?" "Mommy looked in the..."	
	(no response)
"...bathroom." It wasn't there. "Daddy looked in the cupboard." Like a closet. "And I looked under my..."	
	Bed.
"...bed. But we could not find the blanket."	

The observation of different routines among children with varying language abilities suggests that parents establish routines matched to their child's current level of language development. If such is the case, this offers additional support for Ninio and Bruner's theory that the role of the adult in interactions with a young child is one of scaffolding. That is, adults appear to structure interactions so that the child can participate successfully from the beginning, while also expanding the child's role to match the child's growing competence (*168*).

Helping the Child Get Meaning from the Text

In addition to focusing on pictures as a source of meaning, parents can also help children view text as a source of meaning. A simple example is repetition: the child repeats phrases or short sentences after the parent. In sharing a Mother Goose book with her mother, Courtney demonstrates that this is a routine familiar to her.

Courtney's Mother	*Courtney*
"Ding, dong, bell. Pussy's in the well."	
	Kitty cat!
There is the kitty cat. "Who put her in?"	
	Who put her in?
"Little Johnny Green."	Little Johnny Green.
And then what? "Who pulled her out?"	
	Who pulled her out?
"Little Johnny Stout."	Little Johnny Stout.
"What a naughty boy was that, to try to drown poor pussy cat!"	
	Never did him any harm.
"Never did him any harm."	
	Killed the mice in Father's barn.
Yes. "He killed the mice in Father's barn." That's all.	

Courtney's familiarity with this rhyme is evidenced by her offering the last several lines before her mother provided them. Obviously they have played the repetition game with "Pussy's in the Well" before.

Parents can also help children recognize particular words in the text. Teddy's mother, for example, points out the word *truck* when it is highlighted in Crews' *Truck*.

Teddy's Mother	*Teddy*
Oh, boy! What's that about?	
	Truck.
What's it about? That big word says something. See this big word? It says "truck." Look at that big red truck. That says "trucking." My goodness! What does that say? (pointing to another word on the same page)	
	Go.
That says "stop."	
	That says stop.
That says what? (pointing to another word on the same page)	
	Go.
That says "one way."	

Guessing-what-the-word-says appears to be a game with which Teddy (2 years, 5 months) is already familiar. On the next page, Teddy's mother points out the word *truck* again, this time spelling it out as she points to the letters:

Teddy's Mother	*Teddy*
Here is the big red t-r-u-c-k.	
Can you say "truck"?	Truck.
Do you want to turn the page? Let's see what's on the next page. What's that?	

When children are encouraged to focus on words and text by an adult who will interpret the print for them, they soon learn that text represents meaning. They learn that the text "says" something, so they begin trying to reconstruct the author's message. Jeff (4 years, 6 months) notices prominent bits of text himself, without someone pointing them out to him. He wants to know what the text "says."

Jeff's Mother	*Jeff*
	Let's do it again!
Do you want to read that one again?	
Do you like that one?	What does that say?
	(pointing to the title)
"The Very Hungry Caterpillar."	

Although Jeff is still dependent on his mother to interpret text for him, he has begun to search out its meaning on his own.

Encouraging the Child to Behave Like a Reader

One way that scaffolding takes place in parent-child interactions is by the child taking over the parent's role (*37*). When the parent encourages the child to act like a reader, by taking over the parent's role as a model, the child's approximation of reading-like behavior is advanced. This begins, in very simple ways, when children are still quite young. Mia's grandmother asks, "Do you want to hold the book?" Teddy is asked, "Can you turn the page?" and "Do you want to read it to yourself?" Both Mia and Teddy are being encouraged to act like readers. As children gain more experience with books, parents also increase their expectations. Jeff's mother expects him to reproduce the text by looking at picture clues as they read *The Very Hungry Caterpillar:*

Jeff's Mother	*Jeff*
"On Saturday he…" Read this part, okay? "On Saturday he ate through one piece of…"	
	Cake.
"Chocolate cake."	
	Cake. Saturday…
This is all one day. All the same day. Yeah?	
	On Wednesday…
"One ice cream cone." That's all on the same day, honey. "One…"	
	Pickle. One…um…um…cheese.
Right.	One slice of baloney.
"Salami."	
	P'slami. One pop…one pop…popsicle.
"Lollipop."	
	Lollipop.
We don't call them lollipops very much, do we?	
	Cherry cake.
"Cherry pie."	
	Cherry pie. And cherry pickles.
No, that's a sausage.	
	Sausage. And a cupcake. He ate through a watermelon.
"One slice of watermelon. That night he had a…"	
	Tummy ache.
"Stomach," yeah.	

The role Jeff's mother plays in his transition to literacy is an effective one. While she may not know how to "teach reading," she does know how to interact with Jeff as they share books. She, like the other parents observed, knows how to involve her child actively with the meaning represented in both pictures and text. Most effective of all, she treats her child as a reader, encouraging him to "take on the role of a reader."

Conclusion

Parent-child interaction during book sharing is a major source of information about reading for young children in the process of becoming literate. Naturalistic observations of parents sharing books with their preschoolers suggest that parents respond to children's developmental levels in deciding what sort of information to provide them and what to expect of them during book sharing. Parents reflect an awareness of their children's experiential levels as they relate events in books to the children's lives and as they use happenings in books to expand children's knowledge bases.

During book sharing, parents informally impart a variety of information about books and about reading, ranging from how to handle books to how a table of contents functions. In helping children use pictures as a source of meaning, parents often establish conversational routines matched to the children's levels of language development. As children's experiences with books increase, parents help them discover that text, as well as pictures, is a source of meaning. By providing access to meaning in the text, parents give children the data to develop understandings about how reading is done. When parents encourage their children to function as readers during book sharing, expecting progressively closer approximations of reading behavior, children grow toward literacy.

Literacy Environment in the Home and Community

Yetta M. Goodman
Myna M. Haussler

It is Sunday afternoon – the family is together in the living room with the TV on and the Sunday newspaper scattered all around. The oldest child is reading the sports page while Grandfather is reading aloud an annoying newspaper reference to the economy. Another school-age child is alternating among reading the comics, doing his homework, and looking up at TV. Father is making popcorn for everyone. The toddler who has been playing with a building joins her father. Together they read the directions on the package, collect the ingredients, and pop the corn.

In another household, Mom is at the kitchen table sorting through coupon packets which came in the mail. After she marks the coupons, her three children cut them out and put them in a pile. Mom and the kids then file the coupons for further use. Mom's friend is also at the table agonizing over a worker's compensation form – writing, erasing, and exclaiming "What in the world does this mean anyway?"

H ome and community environments play an important role in enabling children to learn to read and write. Many homes and neighborhoods are filled with print which suggests both the function and value of written language. In such an environment children are given the opportunity to learn about reading and writing, and to develop positive attitudes toward literacy. As children observe others reading street signs, billboard advertisements, and other functional print, they soon begin making use of it themselves. When parents drive into McDonald's or Burger King, children enthusiastically read the signs and the menus. Even in remote areas where environmental print is not as readily available, young children read from food containers, household products, and television. They also notice print on their older brothers' and sisters' schoolbus and on the mail truck which delivers and picks up their parents' mail. Even small stores in rural areas feature the latest in video games. When environmental print is functional and important to children, they become aware of the utility of print and begin to use it to make sense of their world (*98*).

Children also develop a knowledge about written language in books and magazines. Some children see adults reading newspapers, ingredients on food packages, or assembly instructions for the new baby stroller. Some children have parents who read stories to them during special quiet times before bedtime or who read the Bible during family devotions. Other children, however, seldom experience these types of print interactions. Some parents operate under severe time constraints, while others have difficulty reading and writing themselves. In all situations, however, children are forming attitudes toward interactions with different kinds and functions of written language.

Familial attitudes, abilities, interests, and uses of print become the context within which children learn to read and write. Children who are read to frequently, who have their questions about environmental print answered, who have books, magazines, newspapers, pencils, and writing paper readily available build a strong foundation for literacy in school.

While schools, in general, have attempted to help parents promote more school-like literacy in their homes, the variety of literacy experiences which promote reading success has not been fully appreciated. As a result, parents whose use of print is less literary but more pragmatic in nature feel distanced from their child's school experiences. As teachers understand and appreciate the diversity of print experiences and the knowledge children bring from home, they will view parents more and more as significant partners in helping children learn to process written language. Likewise, parents who have felt that they could not help will understand the significance of their role in supporting their children's efforts toward literacy.

Parents and teachers who are interested in fostering a greater articulation between the home and school regarding literacy learning might find the following six points helpful.

1. All families offer children knowledge of reading and writing — just the forms are different.
2. Having all kinds of reading and writing matter easily accessible to children is an important aspect of literacy development.
3. Attitudes expressed by family members in the home toward reading and writing have an impact on children's learning.
4. Children learn language that is meaningful and functional to them.
5. Children should not be penalized by the school for coming from a home where more practical, less literary forms of reading and writing are valued and used.
6. Children's oral language and the extension of what they already know about literacy should be the foundation on which school reading and writing programs are built.

What then do children more specifically understand about written language when they enter school?

Children's Knowledge of Print

The knowledge children bring to school of the print found in their environment varies greatly. While print surrounds all children in a literate society such as ours, some children are more aware of it than others. Some ask their parents questions and receive input regarding how print works and its uses. Other children, however, do not seem to pay much attention to the print around them and do not comment on it.

Some parents point out aspects of print to their children; they play games with the print on signs during trips and ask their children to select items from supermarket shelves. Other parents may jot down an important telephone message or complain about the junk mail without making it explicit that either reading or writing is taking place. The parents themselves are usually unaware that these are literacy experiences.

Most children know some things about books. Some know how books are used and how they are read. Some recognize that print (not pictures) tells the story, some understand left-to-right directionality, and some are able to read their favorite stories. Other children can use the language related to print in books such as letter, word, read, title, and author appropriately. Yet knowledge about books varies greatly just as knowledge of print in the environment varies.

Children's knowledge of books comes from their direct experiences. Children who are read to on a daily basis from story books, the Bible, or comic books have different experiences from each other and see different purposes for reading connected print. Likewise, the experiences of these children differ considerably from children whose parents use print only for practical functions, such as filling out forms or taking phone messages. Recent research has shown that it is not only the number of experiences children have with books but the kinds of experiences and the quality of those experiences which influence what they know about reading (223).

Some parents encourage their children to "write" by providing all kinds of writing implements such as pens, pencils, markers, and crayons. They have their children participate in letter writing, shopping lists, and notes on refrigerators. Research (43, 66) has shown that early readers were often early scribblers. Other children may observe their parents' writing experiences but do not participate in many writing experiences themselves.

Parental and sibling attitudes also influence the way young children feel about learning to read and write. Those children who share warm, happy times with family members reading to them or writing together will develop positive attitudes. Those who see adults who are afraid to read or who find writing difficult may also develop fear or resistance to reading and writing.

While children do come to school with varying preschool experiences, they have all begun to form some generalizations about the function and value of written language. These understandings emerge from an interaction with print in their environment. They also know something about the functions of books and magazines and know how they are read. Many children know how to use a pencil, how to make letter-like characters, and even how to write their names. Sensitive teachers can gain much information about students' backgrounds and interests in reading and writing through parent interviews. Classroom teachers must build on and extend that knowledge. Respect for the variety of literacy styles of children and their families is important for extending literacy into the classroom. Starting where the learner is, then, is more than pedagogical jargon: It is a necessity when teachers view children as developing readers not as individuals who have never interacted with print.

Involving Parents Cooperatively

Just as teachers can gain valuable information about their students' knowledge of reading and writing from parents, they can help parents fulfill their role in literacy learning by disseminating appropriate information. The significance of parent participation in children's language learning cannot be overemphasized. They provide early literacy experiences which benefit children once they begin reading and writing at school. They help children use and ask a variety of questions about pictures and print. They provide children with language for talking about written language. They also read their favorite stories over and over and help children write messages to friends and loved ones.

Some parents, however, may not recognize the importance of their role in literacy learning. Those who do understand this significance probably do not know how best to help their children. Parents view formal instruction as the sole means for achieving literacy and so do not appreciate their critical role in providing children with functional literacy events in their homes. Parents may also not recognize the importance of print in the environment and the significance of children's scribblings as they experiment with various writing implements. Most important, parents need to view children's knowledge of signs in the environment, the stories they hear and tell, and their scribbling as developmental aspects of reading and writing and not simply something "cute" that young children do.

Parents need to develop a greater appreciation for the implicit language learning abilities of children. Children learn to process print incidentally through their attempts to read and write. Parents and siblings can help by answering children's questions and discussing their reading and writing with them. Direct teaching is not necessary! In fact, young children apparently learn best through informal teaching episodes.

Informing parents of the importance and nature of their role in their children's literacy learning may be accomplished in a variety of ways. Three specific types of dissemination are presented here: parent conferences, parent meetings, and letters to parents.

Conferences with Parents

Talking to parents in one to one situations is the most personal and probably the least threatening means of communicating ideas regarding literacy development, especially when teachers have good interpersonal relationships established with parents. Teachers must understand that many parents have had negative experiences in school and with learning to read and write. Therefore, parents' views of literacy might not only differ from the teacher's, but also reflect feelings of inadequacy and fear. A parent whose school experiences were negative might be fearful of meeting the child's teacher. Teachers must respect all parents' use of language as well as their knowledge and feelings about literacy if they expect parents to be receptive to specific activities and strategies for improved literacy experiences in the home. Some parents might well feel more comfortable meeting with the teacher at school, while others might prefer meeting in their homes. Teachers and administrators need to be sensitive to the parents' preferences in this regard and plan the location of conferences accordingly.

Communicating with parents should be an ongoing activity throughout the school year, with particular emphasis given just before summer vacation. Children who are read to and interact meaningfully with print during the summer will probably progress better at the beginning of the next school year. The teacher may suggest strategies: Read to your child daily; reflect enjoyment as you read; write notes to your children about something pleasant; involve your child in reading personal letters; plan language games to be played on long automobile trips; involve children in reading maps when taking a trip.

During individual conferences with parents, teachers can also discover the kinds of literacy experiences they have provided for their children. Teachers can then use this information to develop instructional experiences which build on the child's knowledge and use of language. The use of questions such as the following might prove helpful during parent conferences:

Do you think parents should help their children with reading?

What do you do to help your child read better?

Do you or older brothers or sisters read to your child? What kinds of books does your child own?

Does your child point out and name words or letters of the alphabet?

Parent Meetings

Communicating the importance of the cooperation between the home and school in promoting literacy learning may also take place in formal meetings with parents. Parent meetings are usually held at school, but could be held elsewhere to accommodate those who have long distances to travel. Meeting with parents at different times of the day and evening accommodates the busy schedules of working parents. Librarians and administrators might help in offering short term classes for parents with topics such as: "How to Read to Children," "Books Children Will Enjoy," and "Supporting Literacy Learning in the Home." Such meetings give teachers the opportunity to explain the kinds of reading and writing experiences they use in school and how parents can supplement such a program at home.

This type of communication is especially valuable if the parents' view of literacy learning is different from the teacher's. The rationale for such instruction and approaches should be stated in clear and understandable terms that parents can understand and relate to their experiences as a parent and reader. The effectiveness of this cooperative endeavor, however, depends on professional competence, effective communication, and positive interpersonal relationships.

Letters to Parents

Letters and other written forms such as newsletters offer a third way of communicating with parents. This need not be a buildingwide project. Individual teachers can write their own notices inviting parents to school or disseminating concerns or information they want to share. One teacher sent this enticing message home the afternoon before Open House:

PARENTS!

Just as you helped your children learn to talk, to walk, to dress themselves, to know how to cross the road, and a thousand other things, so you can help them learn to read and write.

Every time you read stories to them, give them pencils and paper to write and draw on, answer their questions about stop signs, indicate what is written on the cereal packet, take them out, talk with them about what you are doing and what they are doing, you are helping them become literate.

Children who are helped by their parents are likely to do well. Come to school tomorrow evening to find out more about how to help your children enjoy learning to read and write. We will work together to help your child learn to read and write. Looking forward to meeting you.

(Lonnie McAllister, 1982)

Teachers may also construct and send home a monthly calendar containing daily suggestions to promote literacy development, such as having children read easy recipes or write the grocery list. Special literacy events in relationship to holidays or local community functions may also be highlighted on the calendar. Announcements found in the local newspaper's monthly or weekly events' calendar might also be included to provide information regarding story tellings in the public library, calligraphy exhibits at the art museum, readers' theaters at the local university, or children's authors autographing sessions at the local book store.

A growing number of free or inexpensive pamphlets and handouts are available to schools and teachers for dissemination to parents. Sources for such materials are listed with the references at the end of this volume. These may be distributed at individual conferences or group parent meetings, or sent home with children. Some teachers reproduce professional journal articles for parents, and others have Nancy Larrick's *Encourage Your Child To Read: A Parents' Guide to Children's Reading* available for parents.

Communication between home and school is vital for an increased understanding and expansion of the parents' role in children's literacy development. Teachers who are aware of the need for the interactive role of family members in children's development of reading and writing should provide a variety of support and informational strategies to parents. On the other hand, parents can give teachers insights which will help them improve children's literacy experience at school.

Traditionally, children learn to read and write without teachers and parents being completely aware of the significant role the home environment plays in literacy learning. Because of narrowly conceived school reading programs, literacy learning for some children basically takes place in the home. However, as parents and teachers develop a growing awareness that every environment, whether it be the home, community or school, is an authentic learning environment, the natural linguistic abilities of children to process written language will be tapped as never before. Together, parents and teachers can assume the roles which support the natural functional development of literacy in their children.

Part Two   Role of the Teacher

Overview of the Role

Historically, teachers of reading have looked for detailed instructions concerning the "right way" to teach. Many teachers have been convinced that to teach reading without a manual and other teacherproof materials is beyond their capabilities and would surely trigger student failure and illiteracy.

Teachers must begin seeing themselves as problem solvers and facilitators of language learning rather than dispensers of isolated reading "skills." Not until teachers gain an improved understanding of the reading process and how children learn language – and the political license to implement such ideas – will instruction become more in keeping with children's language processing abilities.

In "Teaching and Language Centered Programs," MaryAnne Hall provides a well documented overview of the teacher's role in a whole language classroom along with recommendations for language centered teaching. Don Holdaway continues the discussion in "Guiding a Natural Process" by relating universal language learning understandings to the classroom and by suggesting external constraints teachers need to consider. Margaret Spencer, in "Nourishing and Sustaining Reading," concludes this section with an indepth discussion of what the teacher has to learn to promote effective learning during the interaction of the learner, teacher, and real text. She also issues a call for teacher researchers and others to record what children actually do when they read and write for their own purposes and intentions in order to provide teachers with information they still need to know.

Teaching and Language Centered Programs

MaryAnne Hall

Teaching is an art—an art so great and so difficult to master that a man or woman can spend a long life at it without realizing much more than his limitations and mistakes, and his distance from the ideal.

—William Lyon Phelps

T eachers are professionals. Teachers are decision makers. Some are undoubtedly gifted in the art of teaching. Just as the arts are not as highly valued in our society as technology, the view of teaching as an art is not as widely accepted as is the perspective that teaching effectiveness can be measured objectively through test results and other quantitative measures. The danger is that teaching built on positive meaningful interactions among students and between teachers and students, teaching that offers extensive language use throughout the curriculum—not just in time periods specifically designated as reading and language arts—and teaching that occurs in a language rich environment may be discounted as less valuable than programs and materials with easily measurable outcomes. If assembly line production is the goal, perhaps output can be measured objectively with some criteria for both quality and quantity control.

All too often, decisions about materials and approaches are made at a "higher level" than the classroom. Teachers are then treated as assembly line workers with a quota to attain in a certain time period. Criterion referenced instruments become the determinants of quality control with little if any attention given to other dimensions of either language or teaching. But teachers are not factory workers or computer programmers nor is learning a matter of standard packaging.

Language centered reading programs based on personal and functional use of both oral and written language require and value teacher insight. The teacher as a knowledgeable professional should be respected as a capable decision maker. Since the teacher, rather than the method, is the crucial variable in achievement, teachers should not be limited to a single set of materials or a single approach. In language centered programs, teachers must go beyond published programs in order to develop and capitalize on children's language potential.

Duffy and Roehler (64) claim, "Classroom teachers do little more than monitor children as they progress through programs." Durkin (68) described teachers as "mentioners" and found that teachers spent more time giving assignments and assessing than instructing. The lack of direct instruction in comprehension coupled with the paucity of explanations on how to teach comprehension in teacher's manuals is cause for concern. Apparently, many teachers are so chained to routine procedures and commercial materials with frequent progress checks and worksheets and workbooks that they neglect comprehension and enrichment activities.

Teachers' knowledge, beliefs, and attitudes toward learners, reading, language, and language learning also affect instructional decisions and practices. Harste and Burke (117) maintain that a teacher's instructional practices reflect a theoretical perspective about reading and language. They reported that a teacher's judgments about students' reading ability based on miscues varied according to whether the teacher had a decoding orientation, a skills orientation, or a whole language orientation. Teachers whose orientation to reading is language based will view reading as a search for meaning and will interpret children's reading behavior accordingly.

Even more significant perhaps than choice of instructional procedures is the teacher's attitude toward and response to children's language use. Studies of the significance of dialect divergence in learning to read have led to the conclusion that it is not the divergent dialect itself that is detrimental. Instead, the teacher's acceptance or rejection of students' language is the key factor influencing learning (96). Allington's investigations (2, 3) of the differences in teachers' treatment of good and poor readers showed that teachers interrupted poor readers more than good readers, and that attention to meaning was typical of teacher interaction with good readers while focus on graphophonic cues characterized teachers' response behavior to poor readers' miscues. Acceptance of children's efforts in oral communication, reading, and written expression is essential if children's communicative competence is to increase.

Children's responses provide significant clues to their strategies for processing language. Matching instruction to individual children requires extensive and constant decision making by teachers. Teachers need encouragement to base instructional decisions on their knowledge and attitudes about language and reading. After reviewing studies of teachers' decision making, Borko, Shavelson, and Stern (25) concluded "that simply making teachers more aware of their decision making strategies may enhance their ability to make more effective instructional decisions" (p. 465). In language based reading programs, teachers' theoretical perspectives and instructional decisions are indeed crucial.

Language Learning and Literacy Learning

Much that is known about the immense amount of language learning young children accomplish in the preschool years has implications for the learning and teaching of reading and writing. Learning to read and write should be natural extensions of these early language learning experiences. Early language learning occurred through extensive interaction with others in a language rich environment which involved much hypothesizing and the use of self correcting strategies. The features of the oral language acquisition process can also characterize the learning of written language. "Learning how to mean" is Halliday's expression (111) for describing the learning of oral language. Learning written language can also be a process of learning how to mean. Yet, much of the direct teaching of literacy (particularly for beginners) is far removed from meaning and from conditions that promote language learning. The teaching of beginning reading has often neglected the concept of function. Halliday (110) has elaborated on the primary, central role of function in oral language acquisition. Yet with written language, function has been largely ignored in instruction which centers on so-called basic vocabulary and letter-sound correspondences. Downing (61) argues that function precedes the learning of form in any complex learning.

Literacy learning for many children starts long before the formal instruction of prereading and beginning reading programs in school settings. In fact, the examination of preschool children's efforts in writing and spelling as well as reading has shown that young children do indeed develop an awareness of written language through encounters with print in natural settings. Studies of young children's writing (19, 46, 117) show convincingly that children are concerned with meanings, albeit egocentric, as they attempt to convey messages through writing. The studies of children's invented spellings (124) show a developmental progression and gradual discovery of the patterns of English orthography. Studies of early readers (43, 66) also reveal the influence of exposure to print at home. Particularly striking is the ease and naturalness with which the early readers master the complexities of reading.

The implications for teaching literacy seem inescapable. Teachers should build instruction on the language learning children bring with them. Classrooms must provide meaningful contexts for reading and writing. These meaningful contexts require much more than the presentation of reading and writing lessons in a specific time period. Print rich classrooms will employ written language as a natural, integral part of all curriculum experiences. The teacher must engage children in reading and writing experiences that focus on communication, and view their attempts in reading and writing as developmental.

Language Learning, Teaching, and Context

Language learning is always contextualized. That context is both linguistic and social or situational. Psycholinguistic research has resulted in the understanding of reading as a language based process in which a reader reconstructs meaning from written language. Small units of language such as letters and words are not carriers of meaning apart from a larger context. Processing written language requires fusing of the semantic, syntactic, and graphophonic cue systems of language.

Not only is the linguistic context of whole language a crucial factor in providing effective instruction, but the situational context of the classroom also has considerable impact on the quality of language learning. In one study (222), the teacher variable was the key factor in influencing the language learning environment for kindergarten children. "High-implementing" teachers provided multiple and varied stimuli for reading and writing in "language- and print-rich" classrooms where opportunities for reading and writing were linked to ongoing classroom activities. In contrast, the classrooms of the "low-implementing" teachers did not offer situations for extensive, meaningful use of written language.

Although teachers usually say that encouraging extensive language use is important, some classrooms offer quite limited communication experiences in teacher directed lessons. Recent research in classroom settings is probing the influence of the school setting on language learning. An ethnographic study (57) of the role of language in one first grade classroom reported "that the language use required of pupils in the classroom was very limited in quantity and purpose and that classroom language use was dominated by teacher talk, largely for explaining and evaluating" (p. 211). A comparison of the language used in the classroom to that used by some of the same subjects at home revealed a much wider "range of language abilities and learning resources developed in out-of-school contexts" (p. 211).

The major difference in addition to the wider range of language forms was in the interaction pattern in different contexts. Interaction at school was usually controlled by the teacher with a limited response by children, while interaction patterns outside of school were quite varied.

Hickman's observational study (126) of children's responses to literature led her to conclude, "it was clear that the teacher had considerable power to influence expressions of response through ability to manipulate the classroom context" (p. 353). Among the conditions that favorably influenced the qualitative aspects of children's responses were "changes in the immediate environment in terms of which books were offered and in what combinations, what materials were available for extension activities and who was encouraged to pursue them, how much discussion took place and at what point" (p. 353). She also reported that the books that generated the most talk and greatest variety of responses were those that teachers had introduced or read to the groups.

Arranging the classroom environment is often mentioned as one of the major considerations in teaching. "Environment" is often interpreted as the actual physical environment and materials. Providing a context for language and reading, however, must be related to activities that encourage children to become actively involved in the use of language to interact, explore, and discover more about their world.

Recommendations for Language Centered Teaching

The recommendations given here are not easy and quick techniques which guarantee immediate success. Instead, the recommendations are broad ones supported by knowledge of how language learning occurs, and ones that teachers can most easily use in integrating the language arts.

The first recommendations apply to prereaders and beginning readers. Children's initial exposure to written language usually occurs before reading instruction in the formal school setting. The idea that print is meaningful is often acquired in the preschool years by being read to; by observing others read and write; and by observing print on signs, product labels, and business establishments. The teacher should acknowledge the importance of these early experiences with print and build upon them to broaden the child's grasp of the concept that written language represents meaning. Heibert's research (128) showed that the print awareness of three, four, and five year olds was closely related to the environmental context of the print. Immersion in a language rich environment — rich in exposure to written as well as oral language — will provide children with an introduction to both the forms and functions of written language. That kindergarten children can learn beginning reading and writing in genuine communication settings has been demonstrated by the research (*222*).

Young children need to experiment with writing just as they experiment with paint and crayons, with blocks, with clay, and with talk. Parents and teachers of young children should recognize that early writing efforts are developmental, just as they recognize early utterances as developmental in oral language acquisition. Children's invented spellings should be promoted instead of being regarded as wrong. The interrelationship between reading and writing begins with the preschooler's experimentation with print, and continues throughout elementary school and beyond.

The language experience approach eases the task of making sense of written language. An obvious strength of the language experience approach is the attention given to the concept that print represents meaning. Another strength of this approach for beginners is the success they feel when rereading their dictation stories. The abundance of meaningful written material in this approach can be a source of information for developing written language awareness and children can also observe the conventions of written language such as word boundaries, left-to-right sequence, punctuation, and capitalization.

When children produce personal materials for reading and writing, their learning is both relevant and lasting. Hough and Nurss (*134*) reported that children from preschool and kindergarten through third grade consistently produced longer stories when asked to tell original stories (i.e., "Tell me a story that you've never heard before") than when asked to tell a story to correspond with pictures and wordless picture books. Graves (*102*) found that children wrote more on unassigned topics than on assigned ones. Stauffer and Hammond (*217*) reported that children wrote longer stories in language experience programs than in basal programs.

Extensive writing should be encouraged at all levels. Valuing of students' writing can be demonstrated by specifically allotting classroom time not only for producing writing but also for talking about writing at peer conferences and student-teacher conferences. Publishing and displaying students' work also encourages children to write. As students write they should be helped to evaluate their work and to realize that the writing process involves more than quickly jotting down some ideas to complete an assignment. Instead, they need to understand that prewriting, drafting, reshaping, polishing, and proofreading are all part of the writing process.

The preceding recommendations require an acceptance of children's existing level of communication in both speech and writing. Positive feedback to children's ideas can promote further exploration. If the primary attention is given to correcting mechanics, the zeal to communicate is dampened. Mechanics can be refined as children revise their work for publication, or as they clarify their thoughts for an oral presentation. Children's language competence grows through continued opportunities to communicate.

A revival of individualized reading with its concepts of self-selection, wide reading of library materials, creative response, and purposeful book sharing seems to be in order. Individualized reading not only results in wider reading by students than in traditional basal programs but should also produce a desire to read. Yet, individualized reading seems to have been discarded from school reading programs except by very committed teachers. One reason for the disappearance is probably directly attributable to the pressure to test and to standardize curriculum.

And, finally, no language arts and reading program can be complete without extensive literature experiences. Literature provides models for writing as well as being essential for developing both interest in reading and awareness of the power of language. The response to literature dimension discussed by Hickman (*126*) has much to offer in deepening insight as well as offering opportunities for extending language use.

Ethnographic research that studies language learning and teaching in the naturalistic setting of actual classrooms is recommended since learning and teaching must be examined in the total context in which they occur. Ethnographic research is needed to examine language learning holistically instead of measuring some identified set of discrete skills (*83*). Descriptions of language based holistic instruction are needed since many of the critical variables of language based programs are missed in studies of teacher effectiveness.

Conclusion

Defining effective teaching is difficult. Even with all the attempts to delineate teacher behaviors, competencies, and knowledge, some qualities of fine teaching elude exact description. Many of the qualities that make child centered and language based programs effective are those that are difficult to identify, describe, and evaluate. In strong language based programs, teachers must be treated as professionals who can be trusted to make instructional decisions based on their knowledge of children, of instruction, of reading, of language, and of how language is learned. In language based classrooms, the teacher is not merely or even primarily a transmitter of knowledge but instead a facilitator who provides a setting where language is the foundation for all learning.

> Good teaching is not solely the business of instructing; it is also the art of influencing another. Primarily, it is the job of uncovering and enlarging native gifts of insight, feeling, and thinking.
>
> —Hughes Mearns

Guiding a Natural Process

Don Holdaway

T he teacher of reading is a skilled attendant to the natural language processing abilities of children. Many of these processes lie beyond complete understanding or control but are nevertheless guaranteed by the amazing learning potential of the young human brain. Many of the most complex things we learn, including our native tongue, we master at an early age without formal instruction.

This developmental learning, which often contrasts with school instruction, is so deeply attested to by human experience that it would be unthinkable to condemn it as inefficient or unhealthy. We have strong reasons to study this contrastive model with special care, not the least of which is our perennial difficulty with literacy instruction. Developmental psychologists such as Piaget, Vygotsky, and Kohlberg have already amassed an imposing body of knowledge in this area. The implications for formal teaching, however, have proved difficult to apply or have been grossly misapplied, perhaps because of the unexamined assumptions of instructional practice. For instance, the illuminating insights about stages of development which have made it possible for us to understand and enrich appropriate behavior have often been perverted into a hustle to accelerate stages—an impatience which lies deep within the unquestioned assumptions of schooling.

Natural Learning and the Role of the Teacher

Taking care not to make a similar error, we may discern in natural learning a number of universal conditions which may be helpful for teachers to consider. First, developmental learning, with its remarkably powerful motivations, does not begin until the learner has observed the important people in his or her environment using the desired skill to fulfill their own genuine life purposes—without the intention to teach. In a fundamental sense, the first function of the developmental "teacher" is to display the genuine utility of the skill in a highly emulative way. In school, then, the first function of the reading teacher would be to display in an emulative way what it is like to be a reader.

Second, developmental learners must find themselves in an environment in which the artifacts of the skill are readily available. Their "at home" attempts to use a bike or a broom, for example, are understood, welcomed, or even invited. This second function of the "teacher" is to set up the environment to invite participation. In school, the reading teacher would supply many books and other examples of functional print for children to read.

Third, the developmental learner attempts the skill in a bumbling cascade of errors which the "teacher" receives with remarkable tolerance, or even delight. The learner's approximating behavior is quite astonishing both in its inception and throughout the months or years that it persists: The learner plays the role of a skill user before having any skill. The learner takes on the self-concept of a user from the very beginning, practicing both under the encouragement of the "teacher" and absolutely independent of the "teacher." The third function of the developmental teacher is to encourage approximations and to provide time for unmonitored and self-regulated practice. The reading teacher in the early stages of schooling would encourage role playing as a reader, would tolerate and enjoy crude approximations of reading a book, and would regard this emergent behavior as the first stage of reading.

Fourth, the learner seeks and accepts help. The "teacher" responds to direct requests for aid and provides it without overwhelming verbalization and moralizing about "how to do it," demonstrating the skill if appropriate. The "teacher" observes the learner sensitively and affectionately and proffers noninvasive assistance, and even when not observing is often at hand or on call while the learner is practicing. The fourth function of the developmental teacher, then, is to provide the exact amount of assistance requested; to observe with sensitivity and appreciation, accurately comprehending the implied needs of the learner, and to intervene in helpful ways, including skilled demonstration, based on sensitive observation. The school implications for reading begin to look a little more familiar: observation, appreciation, intervention and demonstration.

Can literacy be learned in this way? A growing literature affirms the incidence of natural, developmental learning, over a range of degrees, for reading and writing (*43, 66, 226*). Can classroom teachers support literacy development by taking up these roles? Again, a growing literature reports highly successful practice in which classroom teachers have used their professional skills to refine these roles into a powerful structure of literacy education (*130, 156, 162*).

The fifth function of the developmental language teacher is to provide a rich environment of language in use, drawing special attention to a few items of obviously high utility, but keeping the environment absolutely free from anxiety about the "curriculum." In general, an atmosphere of faith and trust extends to an acceptance that the learner will select the majority of the items to practice and master.

Babies follow no artificial order in their language mastery, although one would expect some ordered progression of difficulty. Babies learn in the order of what is personally most functional – getting what they want, giving orders, expressing self and an empathy for others, and asking what things are called (*110*). They begin to plan and organize their behavior by a verbal monologue which increasingly approaches the forms of goal directed thought (*233*). Babies learn nothing without a meaning, utility, or function. We never teach the forms of language before or in isolation from their functions, simply because they would not be learned, which is the classic reason for not discretely teaching particular aspects of language. Nonmeaningful parts or segments of language, such as phonemes, are never taught in isolation from the functional wholes in which they are embedded, yet the brain of the baby sorts out and distinguishes these parts, manipulating them in approximating practice with increasing skill. If those are the basics, baby certainly learns them – but only because they are "taught" within functioning wholes.

A sixth and crucial function of the language teacher is to maximize meaning. A number of things seldom happen in developmental language learning. First, surprisingly little correction occurs, and what does tends to take the form of immediate and noncritical remodelling. The baby displays a natural tendency and desire to become more precise, sometimes asking for help, which is readily supplied. The concept of error plays little part in the behavior of learners or "teachers" – approximation rules the day. Performance is seldom organized into right and wrong, and yet the "teachers" know exactly how to adjust reinforcements and the learner seems to maintain an optimum level of self-correction.

Competition is almost entirely absent. The learner emulates both older exemplar figures and peers. Of course, after several years emulation begins to turn into competition naturally and subtly. Freedom from competition during the formative stages of development brings the skill to a point of hardiness at which successful competition may be possible or helpful.

Talking, once mastered noncompetitively, may all too readily be turned to personal supremacy in maturity.

One feature of language learning which dominates the school environment virtually never occurs in natural learning, and that is invidious comparison. Like meaninglessness, hurtful contrasts seem to be shunned in early, natural learning. Both are incompatible with affection and respect, and both are singularly destructive of skill. How is it that babies react with the same delightful sensitivity, complexity and accurate self-direction of a responsible adult, only to lose these abilities by some strange aberration upon entry to school, regaining them again at some indeterminate stage of later independence?

A seventh function of developmental "teaching" is a strict avoidance of punitive interactions and a highly judicious use of correction as a powerful aid when applied sparingly. The positive corollary of this fundamentally protective function of natural teaching is to encourage the inbuilt drive toward self-correction and self-regulation displayed by the human learner of any age.

In speech learning, babies master the creative, receptive, comprehending task of listening without performing in any overt way. Parents do not say, "Come here, darling, and I'll hear you listen." The natural "teacher" seldom doubts that the baby is learning to listen and observes the behavior and speech of the baby to test learning. Furthermore, talking and listening are in a constant, reciprocal relationship and are never thought of as being different skills. Reading, the creative, receptive, comprehending task in written language, not only becomes an overt performance in the early years of schooling, but also becomes distantly separate from the reciprocal task of writing.

A vital eighth function of the developmental teacher is to select a rich literature in which children will revel and from which they will create a hierarchy of favorites by insistently demanding certain books to be read over and over again. Selection criteria for both teacher and learner are literary in nature. Many favorites will reflect a preference for predictability in language and story, as in cumulative stories such as "The Three Billy Goats Gruff"; many will reflect current cognitive concerns such as the opposites in "Goldilocks," or cultural sequences such as the ordinals in "Ten Little Squirrels." All will be relevant to personal meaning. Most will be written by sensitive children's authors and have the repeatable qualities of genuine literature. Few will be written by educators, and fewer still will have been designed to teach vocabulary or phonics. As in speech, the children will learn form through function.

Finally, natural learning makes proper use of social motivations. Language is the most social of all learning. We master it to become fully human, not to be better than each other. This applies as much to literacy as to oracy.

Fully realized, schooling has tremendous advantages over the modern nuclear household in social learning, but it may also misapply its enormous social forces. Unhappily, it is in instructional reading programs that social forces have been least understood. By its nature, reading is a rather private and isolating activity: Like listening, it develops social power only in proper relationship with complementary aspects of language, through interaction with related arts, and through its ability to propel intellect into activity within the real world. Formal reading programs fail to develop social relevance in each of these ways.

The traditional emphasis on "hearing reading," on testing comprehension, and on seatwork activities – all gross consumers of reading time – limits the social impact of genuine reading at best, and through individual embarrassment or boredom unleashes destructive social forces at worst. There is an urgent need for corporate learning procedures, for active talking and writing stimulated by text, and for the manifold preoccupations which spring from shared literature.

The techniques of "Shared Book Experience" (*130*) were developed in part to capitalize on the economies of social motivation. The use of "big books" and other forms of enlarged print encourages the enjoyment of corporate problem solving in decoding challenging text; the use of group prediction or cloze techniques; the teaching of reading strategies rather than skills; and the integration of language with the related arts. These and many other procedures draw on a rich literature of children's books which powerfully socializes literacy, and are described in the next section.

A Classroom Example

Consider a block of language time spent in a primary classroom organized along developmental lines. What are some of the things a teacher might do? What does such a classroom look like from a procedural point of view? Almost every day, some of the following things will occur.

At an appointed time the children will gather around the teacher's chair near a blackboard, a large easel, and probably an overhead projector. They will be seated comfortably on a carpet or some arrangement of soft furnishings. The teacher (for convenience, let us say a woman) has the children's favorite poems and songs at hand and a new poem printed boldly on a large chart. The warm up begins at a lively pace centered on favorite "big books" which the children choose. Sometimes the children take turns acting as teacher, leading the class, and pointing to the text clearly without obscuring it.

The teacher now introduces the new poem, perhaps reading from a small version in such a way as to cue participation at appropriate points:

> All Over Everything
> School's out, hear them _____ ,
> Pouring down the rain sp _____ .
> On the chairs, on the _____ ,
> Kids all over every _____ .

Alternatively, she may introduce the poem using the overhead projector obscuring part of the text with a cover card as indicated above. Or she may use two sheets of paper to uncover the text as she reads, stopping from time to time for the children to predict on the basis of semantic, structural, or partially exposed graphic cues. Finally, she brings out the large, colorful chart and the class enjoys the poem again following the large print.

Now the teacher asks someone to select a favorite book, sometimes taking her turn to choose: Almost certainly the children will choose one from the collection of "big books" because only special favorites were re-printed in this way. The book will be displayed on the easel with children volunteering to assist in page turning and, perhaps, pointing. The reading will be lively and in unison, unless the story lends itself to taking parts. The class will study some special linguistic features during the reading, perhaps highlighting special words with a cardboard mask or by using one's hands as parentheses. Special attention may be given to a recurring basic sight vocabulary item or to a relevant aspect of phonics within the deeply meaningful and memorable context. These few instructional breaks will be brief and snappy, never interfering with the pleasure and continuity of the story.

Suppose the story were that delightfully cumulative and outrageous story *The Fat Cat* by Jack Kent. The teacher may suggest some extension into writing by choosing a crucial sentence in which words may be substi-tuted to modify meanings:

> Gracious! You are so fat.
> *Heavens!* You are *terribly* fat.
> *Goodness me!* You are *enormously* fat.

Or she may suggest telling or writing a new story about another impudent animal who eats everything in sight. Or she may think the time is right to bring out another wonderful story in the genre such as *The Cock and the Two Gold Coins* by Mikio Ando, for the day's new story.

The children now move freely in the literacy environment of the classroom, reading favorites independently or in pairs, writing a new story, browsing through books in the library corner, listening to a story again in a read along situation at a listening post, dramatizing an old favorite, or role playing teacher in a small group while displaying all the verve of the teacher model. Making a personal book will always be a popular activity during this time with no lack of readers for the copious output.

During this time the teacher moves quietly among the children observing, taking notes, helping, intervening sensitively, acting as an admiring audience for those who wish to share their growing prowess as readers, and generally facilitating activity. She will often introduce children to new books, based on her knowledge of literature and the library. She will not feel that this time is wasted because she is not "teaching"; on the contrary, she knows that the outcomes are extremely valuable both to her and to the children. She comes to know her clients deeply and they develop ever growing trusting relationships. And from the outcomes of this experience, she feeds the longitudinal record file of each child.

At some point, the children come together for the highlight of the day—the new story. The teacher makes this a warm and exciting experience, inviting participation where natural and appropriate, sharing the secrets of how she decodes the print, engaging the children in occasional problem solving or exploring related vocabulary, and so on. But she never allows the story to lose momentum. She is not concerned about taking up every possible teaching opportunity offered by the story, because on subsequent days the children will return to this story as a favorite or even an old favorite, providing her ample opportunity to develop other teaching points about the story and its language. No overriding instruction pressure dampens this enjoyable session.

Before the children move off into related arts and writing activities stimulated by the new story, the teacher may discuss possibilities for painting, drama, making a mural, writing a mirror story (reflecting the original), or just listening to the story again on an audio tape. While the children are engaged in these productive activities the teacher will move among the children observing, taking notes, facilitating, intervening for specific purposes, helping, suggesting, and conversing. Some children will have products at the end of the activity time to share and discuss, to display, or to take home, but they will not be harassed to complete activities: They will be encouraged to work on projects for two or more days if necessary, reworking or editing, and they will not be discouraged from sometimes abandoning what turns out to be a bad start or a "stuck-in-the-middle."

Occasionally the teacher will listen to a child read from a favorite book usually when asked, and sometimes she will monitor reading from a basal reader at the appropriate level for diagnostic purposes. Dated tapes and reading records—including simple miscue studies—will be filed, as will examples of writing and anecdotal notes about each child's broad responses to reading. At any time the teacher will be able to display and discuss a longitudinal record of each child's development and share it with others who are concerned for evaluative and appreciative purposes.

External Constraints

Emphasizing developmental principles about learning, the naturalistic perspective gathers much support from related disciplines in the social sciences. More recently additional insights have come from the helping professions regarding the dominance of self-concept in the processes of learning. Students of naturalism, concerned with restructuring the language learning environment in school, ask a number of fundamental and deeply discomforting questions. In particular, they question the presuppositions of what might be called "traditional industrial schooling" which has emphasized memory and mindlessness in language learning at the expense of cognitive vitality and human dignity.

Few professionals operate under such extreme constraints as do teachers. The effects of their work cannot be understood or evaluated apart from these extreme restrictions upon their proper functions. If their endeavors are to be effective, a significant proportion of their embattled energies must be spent in controlling those conditions which distort or pervert their central purposes. For this reason a discussion of the role of reading teachers must acknowledge the external constraints which can nullify their most efficient instructional efforts.

To take one brief example, we know a great deal now about the effects of institutions—hospitals, psychiatric institutions, orphanages, prisons and schools. Their common features tend to run counter to their humane and professional objectives, especially the objectives of change and learning. All are undergoing current reform at different rates for this very reason. The strict social classes of guardians on the one hand, and compulsory inmates on the other, trumpet the inferiority-superiority relationship to an often brutalizing extent. This suppression of individuality, rules and rituals, and restrictions on choice and decision making, all threaten to subvert the efforts of even the most enlightened and devoted professional. They undermine the most basic conditions for learning, such as motivation, positive reinforcement, comprehension, and self-determination—unless "teachers" compensate with enormous energy, and risk their status among their peers.

One reason for the failure of methods research in providing clear guidelines for teachers, and helpful reforms for young readers, has been the acceptance of these debilitating conditions as necessary to schooling. If among other things, competition, meaninglessness, remedial isolation, and the publication of failure as a result of spurious testing must be accepted, then the teacher's best efforts will be diminished or even negated.

We cannot develop these concerns here, but in addressing ourselves to effective classroom procedures, and in justifying the humanizing models which are used to generate and direct those procedures, our concern is that they should be powerful enough to withstand the irrational forces which crash through classroom walls. The wise teacher will keep a vigilant eye on those social, institutional and cultural forces which destroy the essential conditions for language use and learning. And this teacher will demand that those who control these forces will adapt them to the needs of learning clients rather than use them to organize "inmates" into a neatly ranked and graduationally demoralized market garden.

If the methods teacher paradox is to be solved in this perennially baffling challenge of literacy learning, teachers must claim the professional right to make crucial decisions regarding their clients. The knowledge they need to make such decisions is already being won by new research in language and learning. As informed teachers claim their full professional roles, schools may begin to tap the learning potential of demonstrably competent learners who too often fizz or fail.

All of this may sound suspiciously theoretical and unrealistic if not downright sentimental. However, much has already been achieved in classrooms and schools. In New Zealand an entire national school system of early schooling has responded with eminent success to the needs for sensible and radical reform of the most debilitating impediments to early literacy.

Conclusion

Learning to read is a complex developmental task closely akin to the acquisition of spoken language. Many of our problems as teachers of reading arise from the ease with which, under institutional pressures, we depart from sound developmental principles. The models of successful developmental learning, deeply attested in human experience and more recently in descriptive research, have much to offer in clarifying the nature of our roles.

Human experience is immensely complex and the marvels of the human brain, even that of an infant, lie beyond our full understanding. We do know, however, that the natural force of every human brain is to learn. Faith in the propensity of children to learn, as reflected in our attitudes toward our babbling babies, characterizes the more subtle attitudinal roles which support efficient teaching.

This awesome complexity we face as language teachers is most fully embodied and explored within a wide literature of children's books where the utility of literacy is discovered through choice and response. For this reason our most powerful curriculum in reading will be based on procedures which maximize the interaction of individual learners with an open and attested literature.

Nourishing and Sustaining Reading

Margaret Meek Spencer

"If you ever have to hire a cook," said my Scottish great aunt, "don't look at the certificates. Pick the fattest one. The best cooks like food."

I have never had the means nor the occasion to employ a cook, yet the essence of my great aunt's wisdom applies to discerning good reading teachers. The best are expert readers who read, as musicians play instruments and cooks cook, with a kind of insatiable desire to go on doing it. Their eyes wander to print of all kinds, as if magnetized. They seize occasions to read when others idly sit or stand in trains, buses, waiting rooms, bath tubs, and beds. Like smokers or alcoholics, they lay in supplies for public holidays. They recite passages and phrases, long remembered, from their favorite authors and read aloud to anyone who will listen. In quiet places their many layered pleasure includes losing themselves in a book, a virtual surrender of the provisional boundaries of the self. In texts of fiction or their subject specialties, they either long to be the writer or they set up a critical debate in their heads, as with a well known opponent, consuming text and producing it at one and the same time. You cannot know what they do as you watch them, for they are silent and still. To understand the nature of their activity is to join them in the doing of it.

The apparent gourmandizing of habitual readers conceals intentions no less significant and serious than those of cooks to nourish and sustain, indeed, to keep alive, the mind and heart in the ways, both individual and social, made possible by the consequences of literacy (*100*). In addition, expert readers are impelled by the desire to initiate others into the joyful mystery, to make converts to what we still call literature (popular, serious, or children's) because there the means and ends of reading and writing are most fully realized. They encourage the young in these enterprises as to an adventure full of surprises and rewards.

Successful readers also learn to query the nature and origin of what they read. They interrogate authors and texts, comparing their interpretations with those of other readers in sources as diverse as cartoon captions and academic journals. The ways in which they create meanings from texts are both personal and social, and they seem to know what to include and what to exclude from their previous reading experiences. In all of this they acquire not only literacy but a wide variety of literary competencies related to texts of varying complexity and importance. Above all, they know that they can read, and therefore are free not to think about the process.

Good readers who are also reading teachers are content that their aims should include making children fully literate in a literate society. This gives power and freedom to the next generation to deal with and create its own texts; it includes a reflexive hold on the recorded past. But the simple linking of reading pedagogy with "functional literacy" is an illusion (*100*), a separation of the means and ends of reading and writing. To teach the young to read and write is to go beyond ideas of word recognition, comprehension, information retrieval, and even Frank Smith's famous "reduction of uncertainty" (*210*). Written text is neither speech written down nor the container of detachable information to be taken out. It is the linguistic locus of the meaningful interaction of the reader and the writer—an interaction that includes a hazarding of intentions and proposals for both; for both are "dialoguing" with themselves as they envisage and encounter one another.

These are some of the things that have to be said in order to reject at the outset of this piece both the undervalued and overpaid versions of the role of the reading teacher. The first, called "a coolie" by some editors, is expected to act as the classroom agent of reading experts, located elsewhere, to entice children to perform according to the instructions on the package of reading materials. The second, an entrepreneur, makes the packages and writes the instructions for the users, according to the cognitive psychology currently in favor and the stringencies of the economic situation. English and American schools differ in the amount of freedom they allow teachers in the teaching of reading, but lately "accountability" has increased for both. Whether agent or "expert," reading teachers derive some of their professional importance from the taxpayers' expectations that schools will make their children literate. Compulsory formal education thus confers on teachers and kit makers a kind of hieratic role that carries its own validation, especially when literacy is regarded as "a tool for and spur to higher levels of analytic thinking and formal reasoning" (*210*). No wonder that gatherings of teachers are also jamborees for salespersons who waylay the young and the jaded with promises of success based on a false scientism and a mindless technology that distracts potentially good teachers from the understandings that they can derive from their own practice as readers.

The theme of this chapter is that good reading teachers collaborate with their pupils to gain satisfaction from reading whatever fires and nourishes the intentions, purposes, and desires of both. No learner can read well a text to which the teacher is indifferent. The teacher's distinctive function is to understand, as fully as possible and in ways that no single statement can encompass, the nature of this joint enterprise, including the context of the operation and the kind of text to be read. The day to day practice of pedagogy must not diminish but, instead, must be part of the jouissance (*14*) and the seriousness that impel both partners in this encounter in the first place. Dante, you remember, went on his journey with Virgil whom he admired and longed to imitate and surpass. That must stand for the paradigm of what now follows.

What Teachers Have to Learn

Before they can define their role, good reading teachers have to learn hard lessons, the hardest being the need to make themselves progressively redundant in each aspect of their role as instructor in order to emerge as fellow readers with their pupils. Research (*43, 230, 239*) shows that, while teachers undoubtedly make a difference to the teaching of reading in general, they are not indispensable. Children who want to read can teach themselves by a variety of means. Recent ethnographic, linguistic, and longitudinal studies confirm that the extent to which individuals learn to read and write depends greatly on the role literacy plays in their families, communities, and their jobs (*119*). The recently revised recognition of the parents' role is enhanced by the understanding that literacy needs more practice than modern schools have time for (*162*). Reading teachers know that by the time children come to school, they have already grasped significant reading lessons from their environment.

The first of a teacher's most important responsibilities is to discover the child's early view of the task of reading, for that is what may need to be modified when the child comes to class and meets a reading teacher and a school reading book. Some children may be like Jean-Paul Sartre (*197*) teaching himself to read in his grandfather's study:

> I pretended to read: my eyes followed the black lines without skipping a single one and I told myself the story out loud, taking care to pronounce every syllable. I was discovered—or let myself be discovered: there were cries of admiration and it was decided it was time I was taught the alphabet. I was as zealous as a catechumen; I even gave myself private lessons. I climbed onto my folding bedstead and read Hector Malot's *Sans Famille* which I knew by heart, and half-reading, half-deciphering it, I went through every page one after another; when the last was turned I knew how to read.

This is the reader Kermode (*140*) calls "the insider," beginning a life among books. It is a strong and valid evidence of the joy and effort of the process. In contrast, Torrey's (*230*) pupil, John, recited TV commercials by heart and read labels on the cans in the kitchen with comparable enthusiasm. He seemed "to ask just the right questions in his own mind about the relation of language and print." In their different cultural contexts Jean-Paul and John, and others like them, told themselves that what they saw was what they could already say. John bridged the gap between his spoken and printed form; Jean-Paul used the features of narrative discourse to keep going for a whole book.

Both incidents encourage us to believe that evidence about learning to read may significantly begin in anecdotes, not in test results. What is obvious may, when examined, be less devious than it seems. Teachers learn at the outset to look at what readers actually do so that they do not reject whatever does not fit their own view of what has to be taught. The difficulty for a child's first teacher is to have a view of reading behavior that will accommodate whatever understanding a child coming to school has of the task.

Reading brings profit and pleasure to individuals, but teachers should not ignore the fact that it is also a set of social practices. Reading is "a way of taking" that is "specific to each culture and subculture and socially organized within them" (*48*). Before school, some children know reading as the shared fun of story books, so they expect school reading to include the pleasure of narratives in picture books—as good a way to spend time as watching TV. Others are told that school reading is "work," emphasized by their elders as serious business specific to school. In the teacher's eyes, potentially successful readers come from homes with bookshelves and supportive, literate parents. This view often obscures reading practices in other homes where family stories, local politics, and leisure activities involve the group in significant functions of literacy. Given that teachers often make wrong judgments about the family background of their pupils— in England, for example, quite false intuitions are based on the children's accent and dialect (*231*)—understanding the child's view of the task must precede pedagogy, especially when a teacher meets a class or a child whose culture is clearly different from his or her own.

As an act, reading is neither innocent nor neutral; it is always ideologically and culturally loaded. To see it clearly, teachers have to devise means of making their own culture "anthropologically strange" (*1*) and then they can see the culture of their pupils. This is a difficult idea because teachers are "insiders" who "have read." The practice of "having read" is more exclusive than they realize. Think of how an insider picks up a new book. The act has all the confidence of knowing how to say "How do you do?" at an introduction. How is it learned? Was it ever taught? When insiders say "Jane Eyre" to each other, they recall an old friend, although none of them need have looked at the novel for years. Yet its content and their responses are part of their social reality that reading has shaped. Children discover in their first schools that "to have read" certain books or to know certain stories is to have paid the admission fee to a privileged set. These are the children who read and know the teacher's books and stories. Comic swapping groups or pop music clubs may flourish and show the same signs of exclusiveness and critical skill, but none of these counts as being "inside" in the same way. Reading, in classroom terms, marks readers differently.

The teacher is bound to understand that reading lessons are not all explicit nor confined to classrooms. The sign and symbol systems of the environment tacitly teach the culture. Embedded habits that are approved of and taken for granted also have to be seen in the reading context. If, following psycholinguistic insights, the teacher exhorts a child to "guess" what an unfamiliar word might be, the invitation sounds different to the socially confident than to the socially insecure pupil. Late in my teaching life I discovered that, although most children of age nine know that narrative fictions have distinctive elements of truth and reality (*163*), some children, inexperienced in reading or hearing stories from books, are uneasy about narratives that lack the authentication of a known story teller. They want to know if the story deserves to be believed. A "made up" story that has an author is an unfamiliar idea. Thus, for them, the narratives of some excellent children's writers are confusing not because the text is difficult, but because the conventions of the telling are culturally unfamiliar.

The consequent paradoxes are these. As the result of their early reading prowess, reading instructors are usually successful in the education system. They may be self-taught, and they soon outgrow the need for formal classroom reading lessons. They either forget their early experience or remember it, as Sartre did, as validating what followed. Teachers tend to believe that their own preschool reading was unusual and idiosyncratic; they do not include it in any generalizations they make about children learning to read. They are convinced that children learn to read by being taught in school lessons of the kind that they, the teachers, are trained to impart. They treat as successes the pupils' responses to their instruction and reading "methods." Thus, they are caught between their desire to be skillful professional practitioners and the knowledge that comes from their own experience – that pupils have to be encouraged to believe that, in the end, they teach themselves.

This kind of thinking obscures the real possibility that is teaching: using what the learner knows and can do in order to develop progressive understanding of what can still be mastered. The significant statement of this is Vygotsky's "zone of proximal development," where a child interacts with people in his or her environment and in cooperation with peers in order to grow in the skills they can introduce. Along with Frank Smith's *210*) "reading is learned by reading" we add "in the company of readers with texts to share." What children can do with help, says Vygotsky (*233*), they will next be able to do alone. The teacher's real problem is not to know what that help should always be like, but to discover what will best promote effective learning in the circumstances of the interaction of learner, teacher, and real text.

Debates about what teachers should learn in order to teach have made reading studies into a theoretical battlefield. The worst consequence is that teachers either take less interest in research than they should, or they trust it too much, relinquishing their genuine observations of what children actually do when they read in favor of some process of behavior modification or a set of exercises. This means they have no view of themselves as researchers who might comment on evidence with sense and sensibility. Thus, when significant insights become available, as in the case of the reading studies that followed in the wake of the Chomskyan upturn in linguistics, or the kind of evidence we can now see on videotapes, teachers are not in a position to make use of them as they have no practice in speculation about what counts as evidence. Goodman's contribution (*94*) to reading studies has produced a whole generation of teachers who are free to use their pupils' linguistic competencies as the foundation of their literacy. Yet for every teacher in the English speaking world who has been encouraged by linguistic understanding, at least a hundred are still imprisoned by methodologies that have little resemblance to what accomplished readers actually do.

Teachers like Holdaway (*130*) who have confidently met the philosophers, psychologists, linguists, and sociologists on their own ground and linked what they learned from them with their own understandings of the culture of childhood, the nature of play, and the rituals of children's games and songs, have gained a new understanding of children's relevant competencies. They have used these to select texts that real writers write for the young, thus producing a new pedagogy. Holdaway (*130*) and Goodman and

Burke (99) have transformed the problems of teaching a class with all its individual views of reading and levels of skill and experience into a group event for the generation of shared meanings that are socially built within the culture of a school. With their help, teachers have begun to grasp what a teacher has to know, including what they do not remember being taught.

Between the initiation of a child into literacy and the completion of the school's share in that development, teachers have to practice the habit of continuous hypothetical description of the nature of the reading process itself. They have to be theorists among other theorists. The conditions of this are both simple and demanding. Most classroom teachers take the words of the experts and are seduced into thinking in terms of the epistemology of those who offer them what looks like an instant solution to a practical problem. Reading teachers' vocabularies traduce what they actually see happening when children are invited to behave like readers. They say *readiness, failure, backwardness, method, skill, phonics, sight vocabulary, dyslexia,* and *reading age* as if they were all agreed about their meaning and importance. To take over another's description of reading and teaching is often to absorb uncritically the assumptions behind it. To describe reading genuinely is to begin with an understanding of the development of children's language and where reading and writing fit within it. Then it is possible to see what a child, with help, can actually do to make reading into a meaningful activity. As Richards (*191*) said before reading research became an industry, "We are all learning to read all the time."

The Pupil Defines the Teacher's Role

Learning to read is a combination of what the young can teach themselves by behaving like readers and drawing on their knowledge of language and the world, and the teacher's ability to understand what kind of interaction and intervention can be helpful. We readily believe that literacy involves a looking outward to the society that gives itself instructions in notices, brochures, legal documents, and mail orders. We are also reassured by research that tells us the best single predictor of attainment in literacy after two years of schooling is the extent of the children's own understanding of the purpose and mechanics of literacy at the time when they started school (*239*). We may be tempted to assume that these "purposes and mechanics" are matters of social ease, that they are shared by teachers and pupils, and that children's early awareness of what a book is lies in the ability to turn the pages and to direct their eyes to a line of print. However, we are still only at the beginning of understanding what children think reading is because we persist in asking them questions about the adults' view of it.

Children come to school with different intentions for reading. As we have said, for some it is transactional, in Britton's sense (27), because they have seen it in use in shopping, gardening, model making, cooking, car maintenance, newspapers, and advertisements. Others know it as bedtime tales or TV storying. Teachers making use of research into these activities often disregard something more fundamental: reading as play. Like Jean-Paul and John, children play at reading and make it into what it is—a game with rules. This game they know is narrative—storying in both verse and prose. Narrative has its own conventions that teach the listener and the teller to attend to the meaning that the pattern orders and makes available. Children are involved in narrative from their earliest utterances (7). They combined their knowledge of the rules of storying with imitations of reading behavior. They do what adults seem to be doing when they read—holding books and telling stories. For the young, the silence of the text is the problem, so they monologue either aloud, in the tune of an adult story-teller, or in a whisper. When they do this, they intend what reading intends.

This activity that we call "storying" (163) has within it two aspects of Vygotsky's understanding (234) of intellectual development: play as real, and inner speech. When they monologue while looking at a book or a text, children talk themselves into reading by narrating. They discover that when they tell stories they are free to make up what is not necessarily the case in their lives; they can anticipate what might happen, and go back over what has occurred. Their inner speech is the way by which they grasp how reading "goes inside." The unexplained possibility, offered by the evidence of their early narrations in presleep or play, is that their inner speech is not only a monologue, but a constant dialogue in imagination. The child is both the teller and the told.

As children learn in play to respond to meanings detached from events, so they can turn all the narratives they know from books or stories they have made up into playing at reading, that is, play for real. They play according to the rules of storying, and the rules of looking at a book, thus learning as Vygotsky says "to separate the field of meaning from the visual field." This process includes asking adults "What dat say?" about the book they are looking at, while all the time the meaning is in the story they are making up in their heads.

But stories also have their own rules; once made up they cannot be changed. The print and the pictures stay as they are. So we have children telling their own tale (with variation and embroidery) at great length as they look at a text, and later asking an adult to read a book text which then must be recited in the same form every time.

Despite the evidence of Applebee (7) and others, teachers do not engage deeply enough in children's storying and story play in order to understand its nature and significance. They do not see it as the fundamental meshing of life and literature in children learning to read because the teacher's role is usually defined as doing rather than observing and understanding. We know that narrative is important and should be nurtured. Evidence shows the incredible length and complexity of five year olds' story monologues (84). The complicated interactions of adults and children reading stories together are being sifted for details of the linguistic linkings of text, discussion and understanding not only in mainstream homes but also in nursery schools for children of disadvantaged families (59). All of these make clear the central role of dialogue. Two children looking at a picture book of a house and a family create a story for each other and for the characters on the page. They play the telling of the story. A little girl playing house speaks for each doll, bear, or rabbit and indicates the narrative action in talk with each in turn ("Now we'll go for a walk with Teddy"), supplying at the same time character and motive. She is both author and narrator, as Burnett (31) playing with her doll knew well:

> If someone invites children who play in this way – and few do not – to tell a story, they can sustain the narrative convention without toys or books by dialoguing with a listener, real or imaginary ('You see, then, there came a horse.' 'next,' 'at last'). Their stories show that they understand the *problematic* "nature of events and that listeners are interested when they are made anxious about sequels and outcomes. ("And there was a little girl who was *so* poor that she could not have any supper.")

Gradually, as the dialoguing fuses with other aspects of inner speech, reading and writing for oneself come a step nearer.

The important feature of this dialoguing imagination is what Langer (146) calls "the coherent life of feeling," that gives the motive and energy for this playing for real. So reading – the narrative game with rules in a book – has, for the lucky ones, this strong affective consonance and harmony. Teachers have long since forgotten how "getting into" a story – such an important part of early reading – can be a plunge into new ways of thinking and feeling, and therefore hazardous in the ways that Craig (52) suggests.

When children come to school and reading lessons begin, the interaction of pupil and teacher seems concentrated on the surface structures of the texts: getting the words right, reciting the unproblematic text. Yet below the surface are the child's expectations of serious motives and deep play with complex meanings that are tacitly defining the teacher's role.

Learners long to be perceived as potential readers in the same extensive way as their parents first helped them to become individuals and to make sense of a confusing world. Nothing less will really do. Unfortunately, this is not always quite what the teacher has in mind.

What the Early School Lessons Teach

To extend this discussion may seem to evade the question "What do reading teachers, especially those in first schools or those responsible for the overtly inexperienced readers, actually have to do?" We know that no one method will teach reading to all children. Besides an understanding of language development, the complex pattern of play for real, and the nature of the imagination, what must the teacher's competence demonstrate?

Whatever else happens in early lessons, teachers convey what counts as reading in the school. Their power, as Walkerdine and Sinha (235) say, "is a crucial dimension of the communicative situation," so what they say about reading becomes the reading gospel in that class. What they praise will be appraised. Their disapproval will be avoided. The books they give carry tacit messages of the worth of the recipient. Whatever the teacher says, children will formulate their own views of success and failure. In England basal readers can present a highly competitive business ("I'm on book four; Stephen is only on book three") and soon the parents join in. The lesson is not reading, but how to get through one book in order to get on to the next. In the same way, reading will be construed as saying the word on the flash card, or sounding and blending consonants and vowels if these activities take up reading time.

Our London studies (161) made it clear beyond all doubt that young people who did not learn to read in their first school learned instead how to fail. Our pupils remembered the pain of these early lessons and reported on them with a mixture of cynicism and despair because they had done what they were told and had not been successful. The more they tried to "sound out" the vagaries of English spelling with no idea of making their text into something meaningful, the more their teachers rejected them. "They give you drawing to do," "They kept telling me I was wrong but they never showed me how to get it right." One pupil, when read to, interrogated the author's meaning like a trained critic, yet refused to believe that this was reading in any way whatsoever. From their teachers these pupils learned a passionate anger because reading lessons made them seem stupid, and they resented this more than their failure in literacy.

The teacher's role in early lessons cannot be to teach rules, but only to offer invitations to join an author in a text and to help the beginner to breathe life into the page. If the teacher knows that pictures and print are the source of meaningful messages, then the pupil will expect to be read to, and will, in turn, work meaningfully on the things the teacher asks. When teacher and pupils share a reading experience of a good author or illustrator, the depth of the pictures or the language of the story switches them away from everyday utterances and meanings into the context of feeling of the tale itself, thus linking "once upon a time" with "happily ever after" and holding intact the web of interactions that bind author, teller, and told. If the teller's art is good enough, says Tolkien (228), this creates a secondary world that both teacher and pupil can enter. The text becomes known to the pupil, who learns to predict not only the sense that ordinary language makes, but also the special sense that story language makes.

Good text can be retold and the fire rekindled at each telling, however strange some of the words (orphan, woodcutter, knight, betrothed, loathly) or the ideas generated by the tale itself. Then, one day when the voice on the page is thoroughly familiar, the reader "goes it alone."

Teachers are faced with a choice and the outcome is the crucial reading lesson for every class. They can offer unproblematic text for decoding with the instructions "Do as I say and you will get it right." If this replaces a child's early experience of reading as "play with a book for real" then a parent may suddenly hear the new school reading voice, enunciating each word clearly, "calling back" words that no sensible author would acknowledge. If, however, the child and the teacher together tackle complex text, the child will make great efforts to read well because it is a good story to be reading.

Conclusion

The preceding pages set out the view that the teacher's role is best understood and undertaken by those who practice reading as practitioners: skilled, caring, and expert in the sense of engaging practically in reading acts and arts, and thereby understanding what they are about. They do this to help, in every way possible, any child or adult to learn to read in order to further their experience: actual and visual, social and personal. Wherever the desk may be, the teacher's intellectual stance to this understanding is behind the head of the learner. The teacher's function is to collaborate with the reader and is, in the English sense, tutorial, thus confirming what the pupils can do in this language process and extending their competencies through interaction with texts that make readers of them.

Of course, organizational aspects of this activity loom large in the minds of classroom teachers whose trust in experts is always in proportion to their perceptions of the expert's understanding of practical difficulties. Book supplies, time to read, and knowing well the quality of the texts they offer children are problems not easily dismissed. The seductive certainty of prepacked materials and instructions is hard to exchange for a rolling program of real books, so that even the most creative teachers have been known to lapse into color coding and skills "laboratories." Of the people now in jobs, at least 50 percent handle information daily so there is great pressure to be conscious of "retrieval" methods. Information technology has transformed literacy so that "getting reading right" seems the obvious thing to do. The educational rat race ensures that learning to read has, as its next step, reading to learn. No one offering a view of the teacher's role can neglect or ignore these things, yet I am persuaded that the teachers who best help children to success, who encourage them never to be daunted by any reading task, who can demonstrate that skill is not separate from its use, are those who let no organizational procedure, support system, educational material, test, or exercise take precedence over the encounter of the learner and the book.

Part Three   Role of the Child

Overview of the Role

Children are often perceived as playing a passive role in literacy instruction with the teacher actively dispensing needed information and "skills." This "mind filling" view of learning seems to be inconsistent with what is known about the process of reading and learning to read. Until children become actively involved processing whole language, little learning takes place. Once language is broken down into "teaching units," it ceases to be language and is transformed into linguistic artifacts which become highly abstract and have little to do with the reading process. Children are excellent users of language but encounter great difficulty talking about it or analyzing it as often required in mechanistic exercises and drills. Therefore, children need to be actively involved in processing meaningful print, leaving meta-language and analysis for the linguist.

Smith (*209*) claims that children learn to read by reading, and if they can't read well enough to learn to read, someone must read it for them. In this way, children are given the opportunity of "zeroing in" on meaning as they silently relate their tacit knowledge of aural/oral language rules to the visual patterns they see on the page. Without the child's role of providing the genius for implicitly processing language and the desire to know, learning to read would be impossible.

In "Apprenticeship in the Art of Literacy" and "Children's Quest for Literacy," Forester and McInnes discuss children's natural bent for initiating productive inquiries about text which seems to parallel their responses to oral demonstrations while learning to talk. Forester further illustrates this learning-by-doing phenomenon by referring to beginning readers as apprentices learning their trade; McInnes effectively documents children's remarkable abilities to acquire literacy by interacting creatively with text and other language users in their environment. In "Children Write to Read and Read to Write," DeFord extends the discussion of children's linguistic competence by discussing children's development as readers and writers, emphasizing the relationship between the two.

Apprenticeship in the Art of Literacy

Anne D. Forester

W hen reading is taught as language learning the learners become apprentices in the art of literacy and the classroom becomes a workshop. In that setting, rich in books and writing, the apprentices freely interact with one another and the reading and writing materials. They work on meaningful tasks cooperating with the teacher who, as a master of literacy, demonstrates the many facets of literacy learning and encourages the young reading apprentices to participate in reading, to learn, and to enjoy from the first day of class.

The role of the apprentice is an ancient one and its efficacy is being rediscovered in many fields. In the days of the guilds, the artisans of Europe perfected their skills to levels rarely equalled in the age of trade-schools and machinery. Lawyers, nurses, businesspeople, and teachers all learned and perfected their skills on the job. But learning by doing has not been confined to the realm of work. Infants learn the customs of society and language simply by interacting with people and the environment. Recognizing the significance of this learning by doing phenomenon, Miller (*165*) has referred to initial language learning as an apprenticeship. We tend to overlook the magnitude and complexity of the infant's language learning task because it seems to be accomplished with such natural ease. But the research linguists conducted in the 1960s has revealed the active and creative role of the young apprentice. In the field of music Suzuki's method (*220*) of learning to play the violin and the Kodaly (*143*) system of learning to read music through familiar songs are both based on learning by doing. Likewise, Ornstein and Schroeders's "Superlearning" (*169*), the system of teaching languages based on Lozanov's suggestopedia (*151*), teaches students a new language by talking.

All of these examples share a number of features with learning to read by reading. Learners are active participants in meaningful activities from the start. Though they themselves may contribute only minor skills at first, they are surrounded by the end products they are striving to achieve and they witness accomplished performances all around them. In their activities, all of their senses and motor skills come into play. They are not sitting in rows doing pencil exercises. The young musicians and readers sing, dance, clap, and dramatize while aural/oral language learners put on miniplays to simulate real life applications of their learning, or mime to interpolate what they cannot yet say in their new language. Because learning is fun and productive, voluntary practice becomes an integral part of learning and sharpens skills that at first were merely rough approximations of conventional behavior.

Perhaps the most important characteristic of the apprenticeship is the amount of implicit learning that takes place when compared to traditional instruction. An understanding of the magnitude and significance of implicit learning is the key to understanding the importance of the learner's role in what often seems to be a crude or primitive way of learning. As educators we tend to focus on explicit learning that we can measure and talk about. Yet explicit learning is only the tip of the iceberg, so to speak. Most of the iceberg lies beneath the surface and supports that which is visible. To promote an increased appreciation and understanding of the "submerged" or nonvisual aspects of learning the learner brings to the task, the remainder of this chapter depicts the learner as a creative, composing agent in reading acquisition.

The Learner as Creator

Learning is an act of creating new patterns from familiar ones, whether it be learning to walk, talk, sing, play ball, read, compose, or teach. What we create in our learning may not be novel to others, but true learning — that which can be freely applied in many different ways — is always an act of creation on the part of the learner. No one can tell a baby how to balance his body, shift his weight, use his eyes as guides and move his arms, legs, and feet in order to walk. The simple activity of walking is an intricate balance of a host of skills that need to function harmoniously. Only the walker can draw on previous experience with all the patterns of behavior needed to create that new behavior — walking. In sports, a coach can show the athlete what to do or point to desired outcomes, but only the learner can create the right combination of all of the patterns of perception and movement needed to whack that ball so it will spin in a precise arc to an exact point.

Talking and reading require the very same creativity. Parents and teachers can demonstrate how to talk and read; they can help by emphasizing simple, repetitive patterns to get the young learners started, but no one is sufficiently brilliant to tell someone else how to combine and then apply all those patterns of language. Each learner has to recreate the rules for combining sounds and words in order to communicate. After all, we are not interested in rearing parrots or robots capable only of reproducing exact behaviors. When talking or reading, each new encounter makes different demands: vocabulary, syntax, tone, volume, or imagery need to be adjusted. There are simply not enough explicit rules to teach learners how to respond to and then create each new combination of words or intonation patterns in daily conversation.

To appreciate fully the power of implicit learning, consider how the linguistic competence of a baby enables her to learn to speak by informally observing the world, listening to the flow of language in the environment, and selecting the parts necessary to construct an effective system for communicating wants and needs. While still babbling, she has learned to classify the overall patterns of speech into such categories as questions, exclamations, or demands. Picture yourself trying to explain to a baby the differences between these uses of speech and how to modulate the voice accordingly. Baby not only makes these distinctions but produces the right patterns to elicit responses. Word order is also a highly important aspect of communication; it too is learned implicitly and used in much the same way. Not only does the child use the correct word order, but she is also quite at ease with the seeming inconsistencies that are the bane of explicit teaching. Take the example of the adjective preceding the noun in English: How would you explain that instead of saying "white door" you might say, "I'll paint the door white"?

If you have ever tried to learn a foreign language or attempted to help a foreigner pronounce English correctly, contemplate the magnitude of the learner's role of hearing a flow of language, segmenting it into usable units, and then activating one's speech mechanism to reproduce them with some degree of accuracy. Babies do so through a series of approximations that replicate more closely the speech patterns they hear as time goes on. They test, correct, retest, and correct further until they have learned the conventions of this speech community.

The crucial point of learning lies in the active role learners play while physically and emotionally interacting with a rich and varied environment and synthesizing a vast amount of sensory information into patterns or rules that allow recognition of the many subtle variants in the environment. Based on implicit learning, apprentices replicate and generalize behaviors they have observed on many different occasions in many different ways.

Even computer technology, which has advanced so greatly in recent years, has been unable to produce a machine with the flexibility of self-programing and self-correcting features, comparable to the abstracting-or-ganizing-synthesizing-generating powers of the human brain. Computers need simple yes or no choices to function; humans can accommodate subtle nuances of meanings with an infinite number of language patterns within their control. The computer requires explicit programing— a "teacher" that tells it what to do and how to do it. The human brain functions on the basis of implicit processes to generate memory patterns and activate behaviors. While the computer is limited by the program and programer to a precise range of functioning, the human brain is infinitely adjustable. Computers deal with only the tip of the iceberg that one can see, but the human brain is involved with the much larger nonvisual, submerged position as well.

Composing the Rules

The capacity of the brain to act on implicit suggestions seems infinite. An apprentice learns far more than skills during years of training. Attitudes, standards of performance and ethics, taste, and a feel for the nature and possibilities of the materials used in the trade are imperceptibly integrated with the learner's overall belief system. Apprentice musicians, steeped in an environment of music, enjoy the performances of more advanced performers. They note differing styles of playing the same composition and use the melodies they know as a basis to begin their own work. As the ability to replicate familiar tunes increases, apprentices begin to create their own interpretations or variations. Their proficiency increases as they learn to read musical scores. Moving up from apprentices to journeymen, learners travel to study with new masters to learn yet more skills and styles of performing and then begin to use the combined knowledge, skills, and attitudes to perform as masters.

On the journey toward becoming a master musician, the use of written notations to read music has been but one part. Involvement with and enjoyment of music, dedication to practice and the openness to many styles and ways of performing have contributed more to musicianship than the ability to read notes and scores. Individuals have become accomplished musicians because they built on accumulated knowledge of music and desire to perfect their craft. To them, music is a way of life.

The Reading Apprentice

Like musicianship, literacy encompasses so much more than the acquisition of a few basic skills. The high incidence of functional illiteracy among people who presumably learned to read suggests that somehow these readers have failed to expand and apply their learning. Like many young music students dutifully practicing scales on the piano without a fuller involvement in and appreciation for music, these readers retained their "skills" but found no way of internalizing and then broadening or generalizing their learning to new and changing tasks. Their learning remained external, inflexible, and devoid of the excitement and joy necessary to motivate sustained practice and innovative application. Imagine trying to teach young children to sing by introducing them to isolated notes or brief phrases and requiring that they master these particles of music before permitting them to hear songs, experiment with rhythms, or singing. No doubt you would have reluctant singers and little interest in music.

Learning by doing involves more than simple practice. To become fully literate, the reading apprentice needs to be immersed in an environment where written language is as natural and viable a part of communication as spoken language. Given the opportunity to interact and practice freely with all forms of written language, learners shift roles from passive receivers and rote manipulators of externally provided rules to that of active abstractors of flexible patterns and creative composers of variations on the themes learned. In literacy workshops, reading apprentices proceed toward mastery much like young musicians. Learning to observe, enjoy, and imitate the reading performance of others will be the first step. Many young readers serve that apprenticeship at home.

The more varied, interesting, useful, and enjoyable the reading they hear, the higher will be their level of involvement and participation. Far from being a preliminary or frill, this immersion in written language becomes the very foundation of literacy. Within it, reading apprentices implicitly learn attitudes, standards, and linguistic patterns that will guide their own reading. Though they will be unable to talk about their learning, they will begin to distinguish the variety of patterns and styles dictated by the many uses of print in the classroom. Labels, picture captions, recipes, directions for making things, poems, songs, and stories become the tunes to be enjoyed, taken apart, and rephrased into simple variations of the learner's own invention in both reading and writing. Like the musician, the reading apprentice learns to use rhythms, phrasing, and familiar sentences to help with attempts at simple reading. Patterns within text rather than isolated parts, help apprentices to anticipate and predict.

The penchant of young learners to take things apart to see how they work is encouraged by the wealth of stories, books, and other reading materials around their workshop. Faced with fragments or the stilted language of primers, learners in more structured classrooms find little incentive or encouragement to experiment with the components of print. Far from being neglectful of skill building and practice with the components of reading, the apprenticeship role encourages constant practice but does so in the context of the overall job. When dictating or composing their own writing, the apprentices develop not only a sense for the letter-sound correspondences of English but the more useful knowledge of spelling patterns. Their teacher might eventually tell them rules, labels, silent e's, and all the rest, but only after children are functionally involved as readers and writers. The explicit learning of such information comes after the fact, once the young apprentices have had ample opportunity to use the components or rules. When reading, children apply their knowledge of syntax, style, and story grammars to supplement their knowledge of sight words and letter-sound relationships. The skill practice within the context of the overall task makes for flexibility and ease of accommodating the many complexities of English orthography and composition.

Reading, like music, gains fluency, expression, and versatility through practice. Unlike the piano student working on scales or the reading student completing phonics worksheets, the apprentice reader reads for meaning from the very beginning. Choral or unison reading, enjoying familiar or repetitive stories or nursery rhymes allow even beginners to chime in and "be readers." At first they may engage in pretend reading, memory reading, copying of messages or "helping" the teacher spell. Later they learn to tackle the more difficult tasks of reading unfamiliar texts and composing their own sentences and stories. Whatever the work, they perceive it to be useful and themselves as effective workers. Fears or anxieties about failure are not part of apprenticeship. Learners begin with rough approximations of what they observe and through gradual improvements move closer to mastery. Reading and writing are never divorced from the general activities in class. As a result, reading and writing practice continue throughout the day as children read and write to learn about and enjoy the world about them. The problem of transferring skills never arises.

Apprenticeship implies a move toward both mastery and a lifelong occupation. In their literacy workshops, the reading apprentices take the first steps, and many parents are quick to report that this practice continues at home. Reading for pleasure and learning becomes part of them out of school as well as in school. As the apprentices graduate to the journeyman stage, they learn from many masters: parents, visitors to the classroom, older friends, and other teachers. At that point they also become teachers, aiding younger or less proficient children still in the apprenticeship stage. When interesting and important work needs to be done everyone cooperates and works together harmoniously.

Apprentices also become cocreators of the literacy climate of their workshop classroom. Their own writing and artwork form part of the material used; their questions or interests become the basis for research projects, and their deep involvement with quality stories and poems expresses itself in plays produced, written, costumed, and performed with minimal aid from the teacher. Children bring their own books or those from the library to share with their friends. Bettelheim and Zelan's observation (18) that children want to experience a wide range of feelings in their reading is certainly evidenced by the variation in reading apprentices' choice of literature. Children's creative involvement in purposeful reading and writing activities helps produce a climate of delight which is an essential component of superlearning.

Creativity, independent work, willingness to tackle a new job, and confidence in their ability to progress toward mastery are all part of the apprenticeship role. Learners take charge of their own development and learning (much as they did at home when learning to speak) and interact effectively with those around them. Just as all healthy children learn to speak, so all healthy reading apprentices learn to read, even though it takes some longer than others.

The linguistic competence children bring with them to their trade makes such literacy learning possible. The gradual move from rough approximations through self-correction, to eventual mastery is inherent in the apprenticeship role giving all children the satisfaction and confidence of participating effectively in the overall work of the literacy workshop. What they learn implicitly through their apprenticeship role is that reading and writing are lifelong friends and supporters that are well worth cultivating.

Children's Quest for Literacy

John McInnes

L iteracy learning is an active, creative process. All children invest a large amount of time, ingenuity, and energy inventing language learning strategies for themselves. They are not bound by imitation. They "use the language they hear as examples of language to learn from, not samples of language to learn" (*37*). From infancy, they practice and refine the process of language learning; they do not simply take in and store the products of other language users for imitative use.

Commendable school programs recognize the active role of children in literacy learning and employ, as Piaget suggests, "active methods which give broad scope to the spontaneous research of the child...and require that every new truth to be learned, be rediscovered, or at least reconstructed by the student" (*174*). Children in active school settings do not simply receive knowledge about language, they remake it for themselves. Children in supportive language environments are encouraged and rewarded not just for the language products they display but for engagement in language learning and inventiveness in extending their strategies.

Some first grade children playing in a construction made out of cardboard boxes commented to each other on their "magic boat." One proudly announced, "This magic boat is waterproof, fireproof, holeproof, and everything-proof." When another child got into the crowded boat and wrecked it he said, "I thought you said this boat was everything-proof." "I did," replied the first child, "but I didn't say it was *everybody*-proof." Such language invention could not have occurred in a less supportive setting.

Donaldson (*60*) points out that early ideas about learning assumed that associations were built in mechanical, automatic ways. She says,

> The newer accounts differ from this in the most fundamental way. The primary thing is now held to be the grasp of meaning – the ability to "make sense" of things, and above all to make sense of what people do, which of course includes what people say. On this view, it is the child's ability to interpret situations which make it possible for him, through active processes of hypothesis-testing and inference, to arrive at a knowledge of language.

Recent theory about literacy learning acknowledges the child's role in seeking and making meaning. It suggests that almost all children are equipped to inquire into how language works and to make their knowledge of language a useful part of their lives.

Children who learn to read early do so by making productive inquiries about the print around them. Their earliest demonstrations of print awareness are their guesses about meaning and their "What does it mean?" questions.

Many young readers discover the power of their hypothesizing, testing, and confirming behavior as they learn to read. They develop this power through concrete interactions with the world and through verbal interactions, conversations, dramatic play, and inquiries of various kinds. The risk-taking, exploring child constantly questions. Children employ their hypothesis testing not only to anticipate and confirm what text means, but to anticipate, employ, and test their own strategies in reading.

Schools that assist children in their meaning search and in developing their strategies for getting meaning allow children to use their hypothesizing abilities in learning to read. Children do well in print environments where personal meaning is offered through the use of signs, labels, stories, pictures, notes, and messages. Children confirm their predictions using text and context as much as possible while teachers try to withhold their information and advice as long as possible. Teachers need to be patient with children's attempts to construct meaning and not be too quick in providing words and answers.

Board (*23*) recently documented the miscues of a child whose teacher allowed him to read a whole book, *The Ghost Said Boo* (Gerrard, 1974), without correcting his pronunciation of the word *Claud,* the name of the ghost in the story. The reader gave several poor phonetic approximations on the first page. Knowing these were not real names, he then substituted scary names such as Frankenstein and Dracula. He then resorted to pronoun substitutions to maintain meaning. Finally, toward the end of the book, he arrived at a good approximation of the name. The child was allowed to hypothesize without correction or external confirmation about phonic correspondences, proper names, the gender of the character, and the syntactic appropriateness of the substitutions he made. He remained active in his problem solving attempts while maintaining his efforts to unravel the story using context clues.

Some methodologies for teaching reading inhibit children's hypothesizing attempts. Oral reading situations in which children's miscues are corrected instantly tend to convince children that the teacher, not the text, is the primary source of feedback. If children are deprived of opportunities to correct themselves, they soon abandon the testing-confirming role so essential in the processing of written language. Ironically, good readers are most often allowed the time to infer and confirm while poorer readers are quickly corrected. Discouragement of weaker readers in hypothesizing may account in a large way for their poorer performance. Role expectations displayed by teachers may become the role expectations of the learner.

Santin (*196*) documented the language learning expectations held by four different teachers of trainable mentally retarded children. The teachers' responses varied from correcting children at the word pronunciation level with almost total disregard of context, to facilitating behavior which assumed that the children were attempting to communicate and consequently encouraged a flow of language. The children's language attempts matched their teachers' expectations. Children in the most limiting classroom made fewest attempts to communicate, while children in the most responsive setting constantly used elaborate structures in their attempts to exchange meaning.

Language learning takes place in a network of literacy events that begin at birth and continue for a lifetime. Some of these literacy events are solitary, others social. As children learn alone and in interactions with others they develop remarkable abilities to teach. Thus, language learners learn with, and contribute to, the language learning of others in their language communities.

Some children display remarkable abilities to learn by themselves through play situations in which they talk to pets, toys, and puppets. They invent monologues and dialogues, give instructions, and provide explanations. They also can be observed learning from books and television in relative isolation. They explore these sources of information by themselves for considerable lengths of time.

Most language exploration, however, takes place in interactions with playmates and adults. In studying literary knowledge of four year old children, Verriour (*232*) documented storytelling by young children to different audiences. One four year old told distinctly different versions of *Goldilocks and the Three Bears* to a parent and to a two year old sibling. The child was learning about audience from simple storytelling situations in the home.

Barnes (*9*) clearly identified changes in language development in children as they interacted with peers. He observed how they appeared to be taking other people's existing knowledge into consideration when giving information. Through constant collaborative interactions with peers, children began to build the viewpoints of others into their own in their attempts to communicate clearly. Child-child talk was distinctly different from child-teacher talk.

Children actively seek out human resources and use them in their own language development. They use language in different ways with different audiences. Good school settings provide opportunities for learning with various audiences. Rosen (*194*) is critical of settings in which the teacher is the chief audience:

> In school, it is almost always the teacher who initiates the writing, and who does so by defining a writing task with more or less explicitness. Not only does he define the task but also nominates himself as audience. He is not, however, simply a one-man audience but also the sole arbiter, appraiser, grader, and judge of performance.

Children need to develop their good insights about how to imagine what different audiences need to be told and subsequently shape appropriate messages for and with various audiences.

Children search for meaning through their language interactions with peers. The content of their searches often goes beyond the limited expectations of the classroom, usually deeper than the activity of getting main ideas and details from prescribed texts. Their active searches encompass real questions they ask themselves about themselves and their world as they proceed to humanize themselves. They seek out each other to collaborate in their inquiries. They eagerly join into searches for meaning initiated by a group member. Productive classrooms engage children in open ended, dynamic discussions. Children in these settings extend their roles as collaborative language users. Given opportunities, they are willing and eager to build meaning collaboratively.

Most children display an energetic interest in extending their power in and through language. Halliday (*112*) says, "Language is, for the child, a rich and adaptable instrument for the realization of his intentions, there is hardly any limit to what he can do with it."

Children learning language implicitly know that their stage of language functioning is tentative. They continue to monitor, correct, and refine their strategies as they engage in new experiences with oral and written language. When we say that the child learns to read by reading we understand that such learning is self-regulated, self-motivated, and at any stage relatively sophisticated. In considering speaking, listening, reading, and writing we know that children are by nature "self-improving systems" (*45*).

Children initiate, shape and conclude a wide variety of literacy events for themselves. They instigate the earliest episodes of learning to read when they become curious about print and its relationship to the rest of their environment. In the same way, children also engage in conveying meaning by making marks on paper. On their own, in private, or in the presence of other writers they actively explore writing as a way of shaping meaning. Differences in language learning among children may in a large part be accounted for by the degree and manner in which parents, teachers, and other children respond to their initiatives.

If children are capable of initiating literacy events that satisfy their purposes and intentions, teachers and school curricula should provide experiences which encourage them to perform initiating roles. Within teaching episodes, teachers must observe, respond to, and build on students ideas. In individual conferences about reading and writing, teachers need to take care not to control the language situation to a degree which stifles the child's spontaneous thought and language.

The child's role in literacy events such as reading is to use the imagination actively. In reading a story the child collaborates with the author to make new meaning. Benton (*17*) says that the reader:

> is a performer, an interpreter of a text...he builds a mental stage and fills it with people, scenes, and events that the text offers him...with other images generated from his own individual inclinations and limitations.

The lively imagination draws on elements of past experience. It adjusts to new information in the text. The child's role in reading and writing engagements is often one of projecting, becoming a part of a story very much in the way that the child has projected imaginatively in early play situations.

Children imagine roles for themselves as language users, readers, and writers. When children play at reading and writing, they pretend they can do what adults and older children are doing. Their use of models is dependent on their ability to imagine what it would be like to be a reader or a writer. Later the highly motivated child speculates about what it would be like to be a skilled or distinguished reader or writer. Children are constantly trying on learning roles and shaping images of themselves as learners.

Active, productive language learners set up contextually complete situations in which they learn. For example, when children engage in imaginative play they provide for themselves a scenario and cast of characters. When children read and write they need the benefit of full text to enable understanding.

Schools that provide children reading materials with few contextual cues, or decontextualized print samples such as flash cards, interfere with the learner's natural intent, which is to come to grips with the whole, not a cluster of fragments. The child's task in reading is to compose a version of text which uses all meaning cues available combined with personal background knowledge and language expectations. This composing process demands full text. Writing tasks that ask only for filling in blanks deny children the opportunity of encoding their thoughts into print. Children need the chance to compose fully formed stories, poems, plays, notes, and communications of all kinds.

Many children are alert and develop great independence in language learning before coming to school. They continue to grow in the school environment which offers special resources that are somewhat different from those of the home. Some children meet with failure in school. They become overly dependent on explicit instruction which they and their teachers assume is the most important resource for their development. In some instances schools have developed programs, particularly in reading, that breed dependence, and fail to capitalize on children's language learning abilities.

Many children, though, are fortunate to enter schools that recognize and build on their intentions and linguistic abilities. These schools are marked by having observant teachers who continually inquire into the literacy learning abilities displayed by children. Goodman (*93*) supported such thinking when he stated:

> All children have immense language resources when they enter school. By understanding and respecting and building on the language competence of kids we can make literacy an extension of the natural language learning of children.

Children's roles in literacy learning are dynamic and changing. With a sense of trust and optimism, schools need to describe and build on the linguistic and cognitive resources children bring with them to the literacy task.

Children Write to Read and Read to Write

Diane E. DeFord

R eading and writing are undeniably linked. Readers and writers cannot exist without one another, but the nature of the reading/writing connection in literacy learning is more complex than this simple statement of dependence might indicate. As children learn about written language, they must use reading and writing in situations that invite experimentation. Highly visible print in the environment and opportunities to write are important to literacy learners. One process does not develop before the other, and neither can develop in isolation. Smith (*208*) states that:

> The only source of knowledge sufficiently rich and reliable for learning about written language is the writing already done by others. In other words, one learns to write by reading. The act of writing is critical as one learns to write by reading; our desire to write provides an incentive and direction for learning about writing from reading. But the writing that anyone does must be vastly complemented by reading if it is to achieve anything like the creative and communicative power that written language offers (p. 84).

As I write at this moment, I find I have moved between reading and writing intermittently as I seek to organize my thoughts and clarify my intentions. I read and reread my own message, and I read the writing of others to extend my thinking. As I write, I wrestle with the meaning I wish to communicate, and refine what I have written continuously through this reading/writing cycle. In Smith's description of the relationship between reading and writing, he suggests that the desire to write provides the incentive and direction to learn about writing from reading. Reading also acts as an incentive for writing. In this chapter, I will discuss the role of the child in learning to process written language both as reader and writer and what children learn from and about print. Finally, I will use samples of children's writing to demonstrate the effects diverse classroom contexts have on children's use of the reading and writing processes.

The Role of the Child

The other chapters in this section have described children as active, creative apprentices in their learning about written language; through reading and writing, they construct hypotheses and rules and develop strategies for testing and refining their knowledge. The effectiveness of this learning process lies in the recursiveness of the system and in the ability of children to self-correct.

Two important constructs I want to emphasize: What children do in the name of reading and writing is not idiosyncratic, and the process that children engage in when they read or write is not a pseudoform of the "real" process, it *is* that process (*117*).

Children seek to weed out idiosyncracies in their world as they act upon the world, unless they feel they have no way to approach the problem at hand. In the following example of reading (see Figure 1) of a first grader, K.C. shows how tenacious he is in his search for meaning. K.C. was given the story *The Great Big Enormous Turnip* (*229*). He was asked to read the story out loud without help from the evaluator.

```
           ©One      Ⓐ**  Ⓐ        ©plant**
0101    Once upon a time an old man planted    I hate those beginnings!

              ⓊC) 2. Potato Seed
                    1. turnbold
0102    a little turnip.
                                ⓊC)2.Gow*            *I know that says "ow"
                                     1. G-ow (as in 'cow')
0201    The old man said, "Grow,
           ⓊC) 2.Grow (as in cow)
               1. Gow
0202    grow, little turnip.
           © 2.Grow
              1. Gow seed,
0203    Grow sweet.

                        •   seed
0204    Grow, grow, little turnip.

0205    Grow strong."
                     Grow    & saweet
0301    And the turnip grew up sweet and

                      healthy
0302    strong and big and enormous.
```

Figure 1.   K.C. reading *The Great Big Enormous Turnip* (*229*).

K.C. incorporates a variety of strategies in his reading. He uses his knowledge of how sounds and letters go together ("I know that says 'ow'"), he continues to read and at times omits words to gather more information (turnip), rereads to correct, and uses his knowledge of language and his sense of story to make predictions. When one cue system fails him, he uses others ("healthy" for enormous) to aid him as he continues to read. Throughout the reading of this story, K.C. tries many alternatives for the word "turnip." He tries potato, seed, carrot, and top. When retelling the story, he refers to turnip as something like an onion or a radish. All of these alternatives show his hypotheses as well as his dissatisfaction. He knows they aren't what was printed in the text, but he knows they are similar.

As children write, they have the same types of strategies available to them. They have a sense of how sounds and letters go together, that they can skip what troubles them and continue writing, they can reread and correct what they have left out or insert information they feel might be necessary. Craig (see Figure 2), a first grader, was given a picture to write about by his teacher. He worked carefully with concern for spelling and neatness to form his message.

> "One day there was a koala bear and
> its was
> his name he was going to ride
>   ^
> a plane and he had to get a friend."

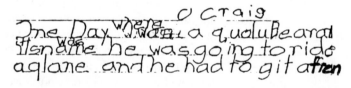

Figure 2. Craig.

During the process, Craig reread his message several times and decided he had left out some important words. He asked his neighbors how to spell "there," but when they didn't know, he looked around the room to see if the word was somewhere on the wall. Finally, he looked in the back of his reading book, found "where," and inserted it. Craig went to his teacher for help at "his name." The teacher wanted him to change "his" to "its" and insert "was" before he wrote the name of the bear. He then picked up where he had left off (omitting the bear's name) and completed what he had started to write on his own. Writing time ended shortly thereafter, and Craig gave his paper to the teacher in an unfinished state.

Both of these samples indicate how purposeful these children's intentions were to create meaning. What may appear as an inappropriate response out of the context of the process is understandable in light of the process constraints and potentials. In both instances, the children were using the reading and writing processes as an adult does, not a "learning about the process process," or one that will be replaced when they become proficient readers and writers. They were able to orchestrate a host of language and contextual cues to do what the task demanded. When we view what children do as a legitimate use of the process, we begin to acknowledge and appreciate what they know rather than chastising them for what they don't know, and we deal with them differently as learners.

What Children Learn From and About Print

If we look at the world of print around us, we find variety of form, redundancy and uniqueness, and a cultural utility of written language (*210*). Smith (*210*) discusses the use of writing in culture as communication, as permanent record and as art. Writing serves to convey information over time and space, to inform or institutionalize, and as an expression of creativity in novels, plays and poetry. While there has been a long history of speculation about the power of the written word to amplify human mental capacities, Scribner and Cole (*202*) concluded that the mental derivatives of literacy are not automatic. Much depends upon how the act of writing is embedded in the culture and the purposes for which it is used. Depending on the oral and literate traditions established within communities and classrooms, the act of writing and its purposes may vary broadly (*119*). Generally, however, there are similar characteristics, or literary links to writing, that children borrow from and improvise upon as they develop as readers and writers. These involve language patterns, literary formats, elements of literature, and literature genres (*32*).

Through exposure to literature, either by reading or being read to, children begin to understand the nature of written materials as being different from and yet similar to oral language. Language patterns such as "Once upon a time" or "There once was" crop up in their written stories and in their oral language. They experience the rhythm of written language as they read and write and play with language through poetry, song, verse, chants and rhymes. Their first attempts at reading and writing draw heavily on this aspect of written language. The two year old who opens a book and babbles "book language" and the young writer who produces lines on a sheet of paper indicate their understanding of the patterns that language exhibits in its most basic sense.

DeFord

As children encounter fiction and nonfiction, they derive larger organizational frameworks from text and understand the use of these materials for varying contexts. Story narratives, content related writing, journals, letters, notes, advertisements and news accounts each employ style, form and organizational structures. These conventions of organization, content and cohesion play an important role in reading and writing strategy development. Concepts such as beginnings, middles, and endings of stories, words of order such as *first, second* and *third,* and indicators of sequence such as *then* and *after* find their way into their story tellings, story reading and writing.

The subtle elements of literature such as plot, theme, setting, characterization, point of view, tone and style develop across encounters with print and feed into children's understanding of genres such as folklore, myths, fantasy and science fiction, realistic and historical fiction, poetry, and nonfiction. These form the basis of the wicked old witches, monsters and mysteries that they weave into the fabric of their stories. The concise organization that is part of this oral and literate tradition is fully a part of their world, before they enter school through television, environmental print (e.g., McDonald's arches) and books. Many families, often without realizing the importance of their bedtime stories (*120, 221*) have set their children quickly into the midst of this tradition.

Very early on, children develop an understanding of concepts of print such as front of the book, back of the book, differentiation of letters from words, left-to-right and top-to-bottom movement of print (*44*) in addition to the above literary links to writing. Even two, three and four year olds begin to understand the mechanics of written language and the conventions of spelling as they learn from the variety of print in their environment (*53, 183*). If the world of print in classrooms draws upon the world of print in the home and community, children have a vast pool of knowledge from which to sample as they begin formal schooling.

Factors Influencing Reading and Writing

While a host of factors can influence how well we read or write, I wish to deal with two that greatly influence children's reading and writing in classrooms: the knowledge and language uses found within the diverse social contexts of various classrooms, and the linguistic constraints and potentials inherent in such settings.

The rules for knowledge and language use are defined within the boundaries of face-to-face interactions (*106, 204*) in given social settings. The nature of conversations and order of speaking are strictly defined in homes and classrooms, just as they are in parliamentary proceedings. We all know when to be silent and when to speak, how to initiate conversations and how to take turns in varying settings (*34, 80, 90, 107*). Problems may arise in classroom settings when the home environments access and use knowledge and language in different ways than the schools do (*51, 119 138*).

Conventions of knowledge and language use influence what teachers define as growth in reading and writing, how they evaluate quality, and therefore, what constitutes worthy instructional materials. This in turn influences what children read and write, and how they go about using the process. If, for example, the teacher believes that children learn by practicing specified forms until mastery occurs, then the social environment will be set up to facilitate practice and mastery. The materials will be sequentially organized, with practice periods built into the day. Tests of a paper and pencil variety will be given to assess mastery levels, and instruction will be geared to results of these tests. The materials used and the pacing of instruction is in the hands of the teacher and the curriculum guide. These beliefs will serve as a frame of reference for the teacher and children as they carry out the work specified within this frame.

A transcription from a videotaped reading lesson in a classroom that is organized in the above manner will serve as an example. Each reading group of 5 to 10 children meets daily for 30 minutes at tables arranged in a semicircle in front of a blackboard. Nearby a chart lists 40 to 60 words. The children sit at their seats with individual writing pads, pencils, erasers and their reading workbooks. The teacher stands in front of the children and moves from them to the chart and the blackboard as the lesson progresses. The other children in the class work quietly at their seats individually writing on worksheets or on assigned story writing, reading workbook pages and practicing graded word lists orally. After completing seat work the children know that they may read from their basal reading books or select a book from the library of "easy to read," controlled vocabulary texts.

Each lesson begins with children reading chorally from the wordlists on chart paper. The number of words read varies with ability, as does the level of difficulty as determined by the basal reading program. The children physically point to the words as they read them three times each. On average, each group reads three to five graded charts. After this practice with previously taught words, the teacher introduces new words as in the following example with the word *naps*.

T: What is the word part? [the t. shows word card 'nap']
C: /Nap/

T: What sound did I add? [holds up 's' next to 'nap']

C: /S/

T: Spell the word parts.

    C: N-a-p, /nap/; s, /s/

T: Spell the word.

C: N-a-p-s, /naps/

T: What is the missing sound? [nap __]

C: /s/

T: Spell and read the word.

C: N-a-p-s, /naps/

T: Write, spell and read the word.

C: All children write the word /naps/ on their independent writing pad.

T: The teacher then moves around the semicircle to examine their written responses and corrects spelling or handwriting. After all children have completed the written response, the teacher holds up the word card and asks the children to proof their writing.

C: N-a-p-s, /naps/ (looking and pointing at the word card)
    N-a-p-s, /naps/ (pointing at their written responses)

T: Spell and read the word while looking at me.

C: N-a-p-s, /naps/

T: Give me a sentence for /naps/.

C1: I take naps everyday.

C2 My sister naps all day .

T: Teacher holds up a sentence card for the children to read:
    "Nip naps on a mat."

C: /Nip naps on a mat./

T: Look at these words. [t. holds up 'nap' and 'naps']
    What letters are the same?

C: N-a-p

T: What sound is the same?

C: /Nap/

T: What letter is different?

C: S

T: What sound is different?

C: /s/

T: Repeat the word after me. [T. holds up each word card individually and the children repeat each word. This occurs five or six times with the teacher changing the order of the card. Then she moves to another word and follows the same procedure.]

Language and knowledge are carefully programed within this classroom. As the above example indicates, at only one point within the reading lesson do the children provide their own language. An ungrammatical sentence is immediately corrected. Except when children are asked to supply their own sentence in reading and writing, or during open discussion around assignments and content subjects or topically assigned writings (see Figure 3), most of the language, both oral and written, is framed by this programed mastery learning approach. The language within this classroom hardly even resembles the language that these children use in their homes.

Generally, the teacher's intention is to teach lessons so that children can learn; often the children's intentions or personal knowledge are not freely expressed in the classroom context. Children may have a range of choices, or little choice, depending on how the teacher organizes lessons. Typically, writing instruction incorporates handwriting practice, grammar instruction, and "creative writing." This creative writing is usually stimulated by story starters and assigned topics. The problem with this method is that children do not provide their own motivation or direction for writing, and therefore, writing may be more difficult. As Graves (*103*) indicates:

> Children who are fed topics, story starters, lead sentences and even opening paragraphs as a steady diet for three or four years, rightfully panic when topics have to come from them. The anxiety is not unlike that of the child whose mother has just turned off the television set. "Now what do I do?" bellows the child. Suddenly their acts depend on them, and they are unused to providing their own motivation and direction.

When children write about topics they know about, they discover the strong link between voice and subject. Graves reports that writers who learn to choose topics well make the most significant growth in both integrating information and writing skills. Examples of letters written in two different first grade classrooms will illustrate this point.

In one classroom, the children were directed to write letters to penpals from another classroom. The teacher had read the letters that were sent from the other class, and together, the teacher and children constructed a framework for them to use in constructing their own letter. The four letters in Figure 4 were typical of the final product from the lesson, even though the teacher tried to build in as many options as possible.

In the second classroom, the teacher tried to build bridges between what children knew and did at home to her own classroom. Compare the above letters with one written by Carrie to a friend that she selected on her own, with her own personal requests for information included (see Figure

1. Is Sam napping?
2. Is Nip napping?
3. Is Ann napping?
4. Is Tab napping?

Curtis
1. Nip sat in a can.
2. Nip pats Tab.
3. Can Nip nap?
4. Sam is potting Nip,

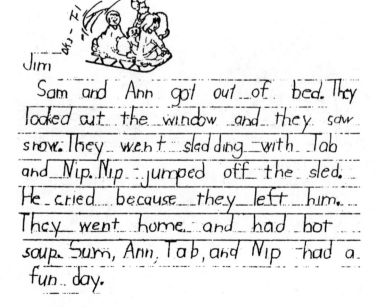

Jim

Sam and Ann got out of bed. They
looked out the window and they saw
snow. They went sledding with Tab
and Nip. Nip jumped off the sled.
He cried because they left him.
They went home and had hot
soup. Sam, Ann, Tab, and Nip had a
fun day.

Figure 3. Sentence and story writing.

Dear Diane, I like playing in the snow.
Hear is what I do. I like sleding in the snow.
Do you like to sled in the snow.
What do you like to do in the snow.
What book are you reading now?
We are reading Beezus and Ramona Signed Kristen

Dear Keely,
I like you. I like Playing In the Snow.
In school we have Played Candy Store.
What book are you reading. Andrea

Figure 4. Penpal letters.

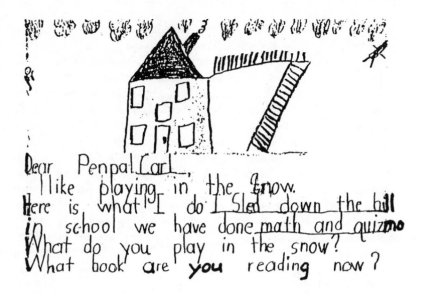

Dear Penpal Carl,
I like playing in the snow.
Here is what I do I Sled down the hill
in school we have done math and quizzmo
What do you play in the snow?
What book are **you** reading now?

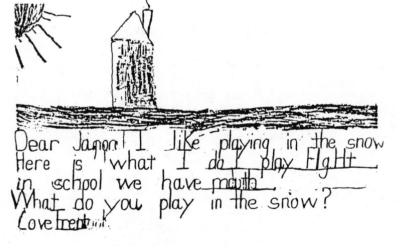

Dear Jason I like playing in the snow
Here is what I do I play FIgHt
in school we have math.
What do you play in the snow?
Love Trent

Carrie's Letter

DEAR CAROL
HOW R YOU DOEG ?
I LoVe You.
I HAVE SAM GIRL
SCOUT COOKies
DID YoU GIT SAM
John ArtHur WIL B 9
ON TUSDAK
I GOT HIM A LEGO SET.
LoVe carrie

4). All of the children's punctuation and spelling are similar, but Carrie's letter has a strong sense of voice. Her ability to use personal information was enhanced by the fact that she knew something about the person she was corresponding with, and had her own purpose in writing the letter. When children use the knowledge and language strengths that are a part of their world, their interactions within the classroom setting are more meaningful. Classroom lessons and experiences that are so contrived that personal knowledge and language are stifled make learning difficult.

Another factor within classroom settings that has an impact on what and how children read and write is the available print. There is a strong tie between print children can see in the learning environment and what they do as writers. If the reading materials are contrived, then the writing children do is contrived. In the samples in Figure 5, the models in the writers' classrooms are very different, as are their written products. Teachers set up contexts for writing differently as well. Except for Jenny and Kristina, who are of average and high abilities as writers, the children are of average ability as determined by the teachers. For the purpose of brevity, these samples are transcribed, with spelling and spacing approximating those the children used.

Story 1
Mark. The witchis wock
ing in the patch. The Kig is
standing in the patch. The
witches cat is black.2. The
witch in her cat wocked pass
the Kig in the patch.3. TheKig
has the witches cat.T he
witches cat scratched the
King.

Story 2
Heather. Once upon a time
there was a bad dragon
he capture. a littl boy
he seb. Help? the boy
escape.be cause the dragon
sneezed. he was happy.

Story 3
Jim and the Beanstalk
by Jenny and Kristina

Early one
Morning Jim
woke up
    out Side
and saw a-great
Plant growing

I'll see how high
it goes And he
began to climb up
The Plant

When he got to The top he
went inside.

when he reacHedTheTop of The
Plant JimSawA cAstle.
"I'm Hungry he sAid. I ll ask
At The castle
for breakfast. I HoPe. They
Have. Some. Cornflakes

Jim ran to theCastle And knockeD
on T he. Door. He WaiteD.
anD. waitedD. until. The door was
Slowly opened By a very old
giant aHa Said The Giant
a boy a nicE Juicy boy Three
fried boys. on a slice of Toast
That's What I usedto en Joy

The GiAnt Shared his breAk
of beef And beer with Jim is your
Name Jack he.asked Nohe said Jim

Don t you have any glasses
Asked Jimonly beer Glasses
Said The GiAnt. I mean reading
SAid Jim. they GoOn your nose

                    Jim cAme down The
                    Tree And TheEr wAs
                    his mother

                            The
                            End
Figure 5.

    In the first classroom, the children know that they will be evaluated
on how accurately they spell vocabulary that has been taught. This provides
a strong incentive for using words that can be spelled correctly rather than
ones that may express intended meaning. Mark's writing is directed by the
teacher's evaluation criteria, and the pictures that represent the beginning,
middle and ending of the assigned story writing exercise. Mark sees his
task as one of picture description rather than story writing (note numbers to
indicate order of pictures). In this instance, the boundaries or the writing
situation constrain Mark's writing.
    In the second classroom, the writers were given a list of words
which the teacher felt the children might encounter as they wrote about the
topic of dragons. The list included words like dragon, cooked, escape, kid-
nap, dinner, stomach, tasty, seasoning, snack, capture, laugh, salt, pepper,
scared, cage, barbecue, and sneeze. The teacher encouraged the children
to create their own stories, using the list of words if they needed to. All of
the stories started with "Once upon a time," and ended with "The End."
Heather wrote her story using this list as a reference and was able to tell a
story with a sense of cause and effect. The listed words, however, were not
always in the grammatical form that she needed. As a writer, Heather did
not always know how to deal with this discrepancy. Because Heather's
teacher uses children's literature to supplement a basal reading program,
the childen seemed to be less tied to a specific vocabulary than the children
in the first classroom. However, all of the samples collected from the
dragon writing lesson show a high frequency of words from the word list.
Obviously, this teacher encourages the children to spell words they aren't
sure of the best way they can, but because she always provides correctly
spelled words for them, they tend to be concerned that they spell correctly.
    The third classroom context is based solely upon children's litera-
ture, and encourages children to work together as authors. The teacher and
other children share books written by adults and children daily. Jenny and
Kristina are using a children's book as a model for their writing. Some of
the events match those in the book, although theirs is a much abbreviated

rendition. These writers use many literary links from their reading effectively within their writing. With natural text as a model, they are better able to communicate beginning, middle and end of their story than was Mark with pictures. Without a specified list of words they feel compelled to use, they freely express their own thoughts. The fact that these writers were collaborating must also be considered. They have an opportunity to share thoughts and pool their knowledge, combining each of their strengths rather than being limited by individual weaknesses.

Conclusion

Every reading and writing event takes place in a social context and has its own potentials and constraints that frame the use of the language processes. Such contextual factors may facilitate or limit the strategies readers and writers have available. This is true of reading and writing in our homes, workplaces, and schools. We must seek to understand the nature of the constraints of various settings and the ways they influence the use of knowledge and language in children's interactions with print so that we don't place barriers in the path of literacy learning. As Bissex (*19*) states about her son:

> When he was five and a half years old, Paul wrote and posted this sign over his workbench-desk: DO NAT DSTRB GNYS AT WRK. The GNYS (genius) at work is our human capacity for language. DO NAT DSTRB is a caution to observe how it works, for the logic by which we teach is not always the logic by which children learn. (p. 199)

Part Four   Role of the Administrator

Overview of the Role

Many administrators seem to assume that the development of a good reading program is analogous to the purchasing of a commercial series of textbooks with their prescribed lessons and accompanying manuals. Often, curriculum committees and teachers also accept this premise, thus minimizing administrators' curricular responsibilities and enabling teachers to teach with a minimal amount of thought and effort. Furthermore, there also seems to be a common belief that such programs incorporate current research findings. Smith (*206*) refutes this:

> Another egregious characteristic of programs in education is their claim to be based upon research. The more elaborate and restrictive the program, the more its developers are likely to assert that its content and successes are validated by empirical evidence while instruction that is based on teacher insight and experience is likely to be dismissed as naive, intuitive, and primitive. "Child-centered" is used as a derogatory label.
>
> However, despite all the claims and assumptions there is no evidence that any child ever learned to read because of a program.

Even so, educators in the United States continue to place great confidence in the effectiveness of prescribed programs, kits and other types of programed materials.

If teachers' overdependence on commercial materials is to be minimized in favor of more professionally responsible behavior, administrators must initiate and facilitate indepth inservice offerings which will generate more effective reading instruction. Curricular change initiated at the grassroots level by classroom teachers too frequently ends with teacher frustration or political insolvency. Hence, administrators have a responsibility for using their influence and leadership abilities to link current reading/language research with teacher understanding/performance and institutional policy making.

Even though Reed, Stratton, and McKenzie describe the administrator's role in their own terms, all three emphasize basic components of effective curriculum development and administrative behavior. Each writer stresses the need for providing informed input, sustaining longterm inservice experiences, eliminating the "we-they syndrome," involving teachers more in the decision making process, and initiating curricular changes at the policy making level.

Emergence of an Administrator

Marilyn D. Reed

O nce upon a time, a decade or so ago, a teacher said to herself, "There has to be more to teaching than telling kids what to learn. They need to explore, experiment, and discover things for themselves" (*193*). So she read and explored and experimented and risked. Most of all, she trusted in the wealth of knowledge each child brought to the learning situation (*203*), and she provided a classroom environment where children could learn more naturally.

Parents of these children were elated—all but a few. How wonderful to have kids excited about going to school—excited about learning! With determination many parents began to read, explore, and eventually circulate petitions. They too were willing to risk. As a result, parents soon requested that the Board of Education allow them to choose this alternative as an option to the more traditional kind of schooling.

And so an alternative program was born. Teachers who were craving to teach in a more child centered environment (*167*) headed for a nearby university and enrolled in workshops and classes to gain new insights and understandings. Interested parents helped gather bookshelves, rugs, soft chairs, and all sorts of materials to donate to the classrooms. And administrators (some dubious, some opposed, some supportive) helped organize and implement this project in addition to all of their other responsibilities.

Fourteen alternative classrooms from three elementary schools functioned alongside traditional classrooms. Classrooms were filled with children's books, which children were encouraged to read. They could read the books of their choice as frequently as they wanted, as long as they got some other work done, too. Children's talk filled the classrooms, as they shared books they had read, discoveries they had made, work they had done. They wrote because of a need to write—a book for others to read, some information to share, a thought to remember. Themes of study evolved which integrated required curriculum and the interests of students and teachers. Teaching and learning became more authentic, more sensible, and more exciting.

In order to give a sense of direction in this new venture one of the teachers was asked to serve as coordinator. She was also expected to lend support and encouragement to all who were involved as they attempted to link their new experiences to learning and developmental theory. Because of the new coordinator's feelings of inadequacy, off she went to study administration and eventually to be certified. Much to her chagrin, what she learned was how educational administration had organized many accountability systems for society and how these systems ignored research that dealt with how children develop and learn. She soon realized that administrators responsible for developing a language arts curriculum in our district had little understanding of language learning. How then was she to bring about informed professionalism and decision making among administrators and teachers? We'll have to learn as we go. What an astonishing idea!

The first thing she concentrated on was counting to ten, an exercise she had used as a teacher. To decondition herself as thinking of her role as the source of knowledge and the director of the classroom, she had learned to count to ten to become a facilitator of learning, to keep from intervening too soon, and to discover that children could think for themselves. Voila! Ninety-nine percent of the time they answered their own questions, found their own answers, or solved their own disagreements and misunderstandings. In following this same pattern in working with teachers, exciting discoveries about purposeful teaching and learning unfolded that might have been squelched with a too quickly stated comment or question.

During that first year, misperceptions by onlookers were evident. Classrooms that encouraged interaction were noisy by traditional standards and therefore labeled "permissive." Combination classes, which resulted from the uneven numbers of students opting for the program, as well as the philosophy that family groupings offered more natural learning experiences, caused concern. Special area teachers claimed that they couldn't teach second and third grade material at the same time. Having some choice in what work to do and when to do it, freedom to move about the room, and being encouraged to ask questions about their learning soon gave the students the reputation of being "weird" — they supposedly only played around and did not work or learn.

"How in the world could a child learn to read in such an environment?" asked suspicious adults. "How can literature books take the place of basal readers and workbooks?" Fortunately, the coordinator had taught many approaches to reading for thirteen years. From her first methods course in reading, where the teacher's guide took seven pages to tell how to teach the word "look," basal readers and reading group procedures seemed dishonest to her. "Words in Color" (241) offered the first phonics instruction she ever had, but more importantly showed the interconnection of writing and reading and of using no reading texts—how wonderful to be freed from a controlled vocabulary. Next came "i.t.a." which demonstrated how much first graders wanted to write and what stories they could generate when they no longer feared spelling incorrectly. Throughout each of these phases, sharing children's literature stimulated the greatest amount of enjoyment and interest. Kids spent lots of time with and learning much from those wonderfully exciting books.

Consequently, the coordinator, from her own experience, quickly sensed and firmly believed that each teacher was a unique individual with specific talents and experiences which would determine the route each would take in facilitating how students would learn to read. Her role as coordinator, then, was to work alongside each teacher in this venture. We all learned together—by doing, reflecting upon that experience, and adjusting accordingly.

Children loved language and learning when they had some ownership in it. To use language surfaced as the way to learn language (27)— hearing new words, thinking new thoughts, questioning, trying new ideas, writing and sharing new creations, discovering the excitement of generating one's own message and putting it into print. Stories began with children's dictation written by the teacher, volunteer, parent, or peer. Early on, the theory that children could read their own language was affirmed. Reading, writing, speaking, thinking, listening, and observing all happened at the same time. The function of language prevailed: meaning and the message the child wished to communicate came first. In the process of writing, spelling, phonics, capitalization, punctuation, and handwriting evolved naturally as each child was developmentally able to deal with them—but never at the expense of the message.

And what was the greatest thrill at the end of the first year (other than the number of parents waiting in line to register for the following year)? Children were reading and writing at their developmental level of "making connections." First grade nonreaders (using the basal text criteria) were read to daily, they dictated and recopied stories regularly, and they were supported with each success, which often occurred in art, when they told their stories through illustrations. They also told stories which were put into print for others to read.

No mention was made of retention because they had not completed "the first grade requirements." Their development wires were not yet ready to connect, but their teachers knew a little more time and nurturing would enable that to happen. How right they were! All were readers in second grade, and some today are honor students. The quick readers were reading books on whatever level interested them, and never had to "stay with the boring group." Each child was nurtured on his/her own personal timetable. In jargon terms, the alternative classrooms were nongraded except for chronological age assignments for administrative convenience and parental/community security.

This transition year was exhilarating and exhausting for the teachers. One teacher said, "I know more about a child reading with him only a few minutes a day than I ever knew about him in a group. He reads from his book and his writing, he asks questions and seeks help from another child – no, that's not cheating! Being aware of his actions and interactions gives me far more insight into his learning than I ever knew was possible."

"But how can you ever keep track of what every child is doing?" the teachers were asked. The responses were a potpourri of record keeping that documented each child's growth. Most important was keeping some of each child's work and notations of various responses. All agreed this was not as neat and tidy as checking off how many beginning sounds a child got wrong on a worksheet, but it was more honest. The following examples of Joel's informational writing, done without adult help, in October compared with his January writing exemplifies his growth in sound-symbol relationships; improved accuracy with reversals; an increased vocabulary; more direct input in class discussions and sharing; and a flow of thoughts rather than repetitive listing, as well as development in invented spelling and handwriting.

I S๑๑ How SIS
I S๑๑ 9uci? in +H๑ Hwosis
I S๑๑ gRaS N๑g +H๑ HowSiS
Sum R wit anD Sum R g๑๑n HowSiS   (October)

ther are 9 9laenet? tHe I SiD uva
the Earth is Moring the uthr sip is nit
the zun is a star
Armstrong wuz the 9r st to walk (January)
on the moon.

Writing a message that makes sense to the writer is more authentic than everyone having practice dittoes to correct letter reversals. The learner gradually standardizes these mechanics through use in context while the generated message always takes priority.

Literature books were always the base of the language program (136). Classrooms were full of books – picture books, easy-to-read books, poetry, fantasy, realistic fiction, historical fiction, biography, and informational books. The school provided some, teachers purchased many, and most teachers regularly brought in books from three or four libraries. Books related to the ongoing theme of study (*187*) were prominent as well as books centered around study of a component of literature such as a genre, author, illustrator, and so forth. Reading was a top priority. In addition to Sustained Silent Reading (*156*) each teacher read aloud daily. And reading was chosen by students as a part of work time, as opposed to only reading library books when all other work was done.

A sustained quiet time for kids to write soon followed. Journal writing also developed more each year as research supported its importance and as teachers became more convinced of its authenticity and skilled in facilitating the process. The importance of beginning with a first draft followed by successive drafts to revise the message and to edit the surface errors (punctuation, spelling) has evolved through the years.

Thought ramblings also surfaced. One teacher began capitalizing on this concept, and it has continued ever since. Somehow, composing seemed less risky when thoughts could "ramble" on to paper. This became kids' and teachers' personal writing: Describing one's feelings, painting pictures with words, thinking through thoughts on paper, releasing some inner concerns or exhilarating joys. "Thought Ramblings" also became the title of a newsletter to parents.

Providing children with a rich environment in which learning could flourish, the staff was continually amazed with the implicit learning abilities of children. After leading a three day conference on the Piagetian theory of child development (*73, 74*), David Elkind consented to serve as a consultant to the alternative staff for two extra days. We gained additional insights into ways children learn and how the limited structure of traditional education constrained their natural development. *Leo the Late Bloomer* (Kraus, 1971), *Frederick* (Lionni, 1967), *A Pocketful of Cricket* (Caudill, 1964), and *Sam, Bangs, and Moonshine* (Ness, 1966) took on new meaning.

Even though parents were supportive of developmental instruction, many still had questions. "Why isn't my child bringing home any papers?" (No workbook pages and very few dittoes.) "How can we be sure our kids will learn without reading groups and spelling tests?" They needed reassurance. And so we provided a program in which parents became the active learners in this new process of learning (*186*). They explored several classroom environments, and did several assignments which included opportunities for choice and pursuit of personal interests. This simulated experience stimulated the following comments from participating parents:

> "I've worked harder on this than I ever did when I was in school."
> "Now I know why lots of paper don't come home—all my work is on this display!"
> "It's such fun learning from each other. We all chose different things."

Only one parent fulfilled the assigned expectations: Others chose to do parts of the assignment in more depth and in a way that was personal for them.

"I just couldn't get any writing done so I typed up a conversation I had with my husband about the exciting feelings I had in class last week." Another parent shared her learnings in a graphic display, another wrote and illustrated a beautiful "thought rambling," and yet another "was so filled with feelings I just had to write" (pages and pages). Each apologized for not completing all parts of the assignment, but each was supported for what had been accomplished and for creative thinking. Where each of them "was" as learners became the starting point, and they were guided to explore areas they had not touched. Learning started with strengths and success. They learned by doing rather than by being told.

Because most parents had experienced traditional schooling, they continually needed help in understanding the fragmentation of their learning and the wholeness of their children's learning. The most helpful analogy proved to be the comparison of school learning and life learning. Only in school learning are skills and concepts separated. All disciplines are used in "real" learning, such as when we learn to cook, drive a car, build a house, or run a business. The context of learning or doing determines what interrelated skills or concepts are needed to be learned or used. Newsletters to parents discussed how "the basics" were woven together in holistic learning to help them make connections between their own learning experience and those of their children.

After a few years of implementing the alternative program, the staff realized that the per pupil money for reading texts was being spent for basal readers and workbooks in the traditional program, but not in the alternative program because basals were not used. Hastily, we prepared a list of hundreds of books which we adopted as texts for the alternative program. Each teacher listed titles for his/her classroom. The result was a breadth of titles with very little overlap. Thus, students had a choice of hundreds of books.

When these books first arrived in the school office, pandemonium broke out. Everyone was reading books—the secretary, the nurse, the custodian, the principal, the cooks, and any teacher who happened by. The question, "Where did these neat books come from?" followed. The fact that these books were for the alternative program was received with mixed emotions—conventional teachers wondered why they couldn't have them, too. Another question raised was, "But shouldn't there be a list of books every child must read?" But with each attempt to agree upon the list, there was never really enough time to pursue it or evidence that agreement could be reached. So kids kept reading books and by their own choosing most of them completed a wide variety.

The staff of the alternative program continually sought deeper understanding of literature and the language arts through workshops and conferences, as well as graduate work at the university. They also asked for help in science which culminated in a week long oceanography/photography study on Andros Island—at their own expense. Courses in Children's Literature were arranged with a nearby university to acquaint staff members with new titles and help deepen their understanding of different genres and other components of literature. Courses were offered in poetry, fantasy, adolescent literature, literature for early childhood, the art of picture books, historical fiction, the history of children's literature, and literature for primary and intermediate grades.

In addition to these inservice efforts, the coordinator met with each staff member at the beginning of each year to discuss specific needs. The most frequent request each fall is for the coordinator to visit the classroom and follow up with a conference at least once a month. Unfortunately, every June the main criticism is that the coordinator hasn't honored that request. What a struggle it is to keep this as a first priority, not allowing bureaucratic trivia to interfere. Why do these teachers want their coordinator—and evaluator—in their classrooms?

Because she honestly respects the uniqueness of each teacher, the teachers trust the coordinator. The staff knows she is another pair of ears and eyes that can observe and listen from a different vantage point. Some teachers have specific activities or behaviors they want observed, while others want support for things well done and constructive criticism for improvement. Conference time is a time for reflection for both teacher and supervisor.

After five years' involvement in this alternative program, the coordinator entered a doctoral program, beginning four years of study into the theory of language arts, informal education, and administration. How encouraging it was to read research studies that supported the ideas being implemented in our alternative classrooms. For example, Halliday (*111*) and Chomsky (*40*) pointed out the importance of children interacting with peers, teachers, and materials. (Yes, talking to oneself has merit, too!) The need for reading to children in the home, as well as daily book experiences in the classroom, has been well documented. More recently, Applebee (*7*) demonstrated the effect that exposure to quality literature over a long period of time has on children's concept of story and story recall. The effect of these book experiences becomes apparent in children's writing. Additionally, such literacy experiences deepen children's understanding of their real world and the worlds of imagination beyond that. Reading comes naturally if we involve children appropriately with quality books.

The work of Moffett (*166*), Graves (*101*), King (*142*), and Clay, encouraged the function, development, and process of writing – while traditionalists kept emphasizing the "form" of writing. Read's categorizations of speech sounds (*184*) demonstrated that the children's natural writing and spelling had merit. Smith (*207*) suggested that learning to read must go beyond rote learning: Children are not empty vessels into which teachers pour selected skills and nuggets of learning; they must relate situations they find themselves in to prior knowledge to make sense rather than nonsense. Thus, joy that comes from reading relevant stories and poems, the need for creativity, the nurturing of the imagination, feelings about what is read, the relationship of the reader to the text, and the significance of experiencing the many types of literature make significant contributions to an enriching language arts program.

The role of the teacher as facilitator rather than director of learning was upheld by Goodman (*91*) and by Bussis, Chittenden, and Amarel (*33*). Research on learning styles (*65*) and on brain hemispheres (*79*), meshed well with data from Piaget (*173*), lending support for active learning as well as the interrelatedness of all learning.

This interest in linking theory to the alternative program led to the coordinator's own research (*185*). Feeling an obligation to document the effectiveness of the alternative program without threatening the staff in any program, she interviewed a random sample of second and fifth grade students and teachers in the traditional and alternative programs to determine what their reactions were to books that were read aloud. There were two major findings from students' reactions. 1) The more exposure to literature the children had, the more they initiated reading on their own, wanted the experiences of read aloud books continued at school and at home, wrote stories on their own, established quality lifelong reading practices, and felt they had learned from books read aloud. 2) The more ownership or active involvement students had in the read aloud experiences, the more they felt they learned.

Although all the teachers read aloud to their students, their priorities and purposes for reading books aloud were different. Traditional teachers saw this time as set apart from the regular curriculum, did not read as often or for as long a time as the alternative teachers, and looked more for "right" answers and lessons children should learn. On the other hand, informal classroom teachers felt that reading books aloud was an integral and important part of their total program, and they encouraged children's reactions and individual restructuring of thinking.

Informal teachers overall had a deeper sense of the educative power of literature which was the base of their reading program.

Another role of the coordinator was working with liaisons at a nearby university to ensure continued staff development. These connections made it possible for university faculty to work with alternative program staff and students: The professors brought the theory and the alternative classrooms provided the practice. Without the help of a couple of university professors, when discouragement prevailed, the alternative program would never have survived. They stretched the staff and coordinator to dimensions never believed reachable.

Another service the university provided was the placement of many education students from an alternative preservice program in the informal classrooms throughout the year. This program known as EPIC (Educational Program for Integrative Curriculum) has supplied many of the teachers on the alternative staff. Such programs are the hope for education today. These teachers never had to unlearn the false security of a basal text approach to reading and the limitations it puts on learning the other components of the language arts.

And did they all live happily ever after? Parents continue to support a growing program—in a declining total school environment. Top quality teachers who truly believe in the philosophy continue with the program, continue to seek new knowledge, and are the crucial element to its success. The Board of Education and Central Office Administration continue to support the alternative program. The alternative has allowed opportunities otherwise prohibited, such as a literature based reading/language program in place of the required textbook approach. Colleagues from the university continue to work with the staff and students, which greatly enhances the program. Last, the role of the coordinator seems to have been a necessary one: to be a supporter; to run interference; to remind all involved that improved instruction takes a long time and requires a great deal of effort; to discover and affirm that diversity of staff, students, and curriculum is perhaps our greatest strength; to continue learning; to keep the dream alive; and to keep dreaming of the unending possibilities for exciting and meaningful teaching and learning.

Removing the "We-They" Syndrome

G. William Stratton

Y ears ago, when I was a beginning teacher in an Ottawa secondary
school, "Chubby" Atkinson was my principal. I have to call him
Chubby because I can't remember his real name; everyone called him
Chubby. He was a jovial cherub who hobbled around with the help of two
canes. The school was large and old, so old that it had three floors and each
room had a front and back door. At least once a week, Chubby made a tour
of the classrooms. I became so accustomed to Chubby's limping in the back
door of my third floor room that I rarely noted his arrival or departure.

One day, I was vaguely aware that he had hobbled into the room but
I continued teaching Conrad's *Youth*. Suddenly, I saw a pudgy hand raised
from a desk in the middle of the room. Gulp! "Yes, Mr. Atkinson?" "I don't
agree with the last point you made." Several gulps. "Why, Mr. Atkinson,
sir?" Chubby then gave a terse objection to the point and sat back to see
how I would handle the situation. I didn't. Immediately, several hands shot
up and my fabulous grade eleven students quietly but firmly pointed out to
their principal that if he took this passage or those comments into account
then the point was perfectly valid. The discussion raged for the rest of the
period. I stood, arms folded, and listened. After twenty minutes, Chubby
stood and said, "I enjoyed that. I'll be back tomorrow."

He became part of the class for the next four or five periods. He
hobbled in with the class, sat in the same desk, and took his turn answering
questions or making comments. (In those days, the teacher directed lesson
was the only way one taught.) The class and I were disappointed when he
could no longer attend our class.

I use Chubby to illustrate some points about the role of the principal
as administrator in the teaching of reading. First, we never cease learning
how to read. The students were learning how to come to grips with a dense
Conradian text. And Chubby helped them to learn to read, whether he
knew it or not.

And students also learned that a man who had suffered trench foot in World War I and was a Latin and Greek scholar read a story differently from a young whippersnapper recently graduated from college. They learned that their own reaction to a text was just as valid as Atkinson's or Stratton's and that literature depends a great deal on what the reader brings to the text. They learned that connotation can never be stable but will shift within the text and from reader to reader. And finally they learned that working hard on a text can be fun. (Their teacher learned a lot, too.)

Chubby in the classroom is the best and most effective way an administrator can help in teaching children to read and helping teachers to become more effective. Perhaps we should call it the "Chubby Method." The frequent visitation to a classroom, the constant interaction with teacher and students, the deepening familiarity with personnel and program, all help an administrator help students and teachers.

Chubby was lucky, though. He had only one school, about 1,200 students, and approximately seventy teachers. With diligence, he could manage the Chubby Method. Multiply the school by ten and only a hero of mythical proportions can accomplish the feat. Multiply it by a hundred and even a staff of ten consultants cannot do it. Etobicoke, where I work, has roughly eighty times the number of schools that Chubby had to deal with. An English department of three consultants and one coordinator can indulge in the Chubby Method only rarely.

In Etobicoke, Helen may work with a kindergarten teacher, help organize the room, and work with and observe the children for, perhaps, a week, and then not return to that room for months. For several days in a row, Ruth may help a teacher set up a beginning reading program in Grade 1 and then be forced to leave until that teacher calls for more help. Gillda may help a Grade 6 or Grade 10 teacher select novels and set up a program for group study and then, reluctantly, leave teacher and class alone, except for infrequent visits. As coordinator, I am tied more closely to my desk than are the consultants and can use the Chubby Method even less than they. We are all convinced that the Chubby Method is the best way, but we have had to devise other means, none of them original, but most of them effective.

One of the most important things an administrator must do to help teachers is one that many teachers distrust. Administrators, or some of them, must keep abreast of current research, successful classroom practices, and recent thoughts about teaching and learning. Most classroom teachers tend to dismiss this kind of knowledge with an impatient shrug. "Don't give us theory," they cry, "give us something practical we can do in the classroom tomorrow." They are right, of course, but they are also wrong. A few cry "practical," when they mean "gimmicky." A few others want busywork which will help them survive. Some have tried, or half tried, new ideas and found them wanting. But most classroom teachers are loath to admit that nothing is so practical as a good theory.

So the administrator, once he or she has assimilated, evaluated and tested (in classrooms) theory, must find ways of presenting new ideas to teachers. Whatever they are, the administrator must present new ideas to most teachers with care. Contrary to popular conviction, teachers are human. To cling to what has always been done is human; to move on to what will surely work but will take effort to implement is exceptional.

The best way to convince many teachers of the value in new ideas is to have the theorists themselves present their concepts to the teachers. Then the teachers discover that the theorists are human and have actually spent years testing the concepts in classrooms. The newfangled then becomes the obvious and the practical.

The director and superintendents of my jurisdiction have been very generous in supporting invitations to recognized authorities from around the world. Most of these invitations have been accepted and the teachers of the borough have had the opportunity to attend sessions presented by top notch theorists and practitioners.

These speakers act as catalysts for teachers and administrators. But they are here for a brief period of time, and we are left to implement their ideas. One of the ways we implement what we learn is through writing guidelines. These guidelines not only reflect recent knowledge about language and teaching but they also reflect and extend policy statements set down by the Ontario Ministry of Education. Fortunately, the ministry policy statements are sound and based, for the most part, on fairly recent research and knowledge. The ministry yoke is easy and its burden light for us. We administrators, especially consultants, continually interpret policy to teachers and help them put it into practice.

The Etobicoke reading guidelines were developed soon after a three day visit from Ken and Yetta Goodman and after many lectures at the Ontario Institute for Studies in Education by Frank Smith. The guidelines were not built merely on that basis, though. Consultants had worked with teachers and classes so that the guideline writers knew how those concepts would work in the classroom. Classroom teachers also helped write the guidelines and rigorously evaluated them before they were printed for use in the schools.

The guidelines for teaching writing were begun before the reading guidelines, but a major shift in their emphasis and direction took place about five years ago. The first cause of this shift, that of emphasis upon process rather than product, was the publication of the Bullock Report in Britain (30). The second cause was the teaching of Jimmy Britton (University of London) when he visited OISE for a year. The third, and most dramatic, cause of the shift was two visits of three days each by Donald Graves of the University of New Hampshire.

The new writing guidelines, like the reading guidelines, were produced only after consultants and the coordinator worked with teachers in the classrooms from Kindergarten to Grade 13.

The reading and writing guidelines are still being produced and revised and are gradually being implemented. One of the best ways to implement guidelines is to give as many teachers as possible an overview of the new concepts, processes, and procedures in the guideline and then wait for their requests to have consultants visit their classrooms to help implement certain aspects of the guidelines. The period of waiting for teachers to call is not an empty time. During that period, and during the time of consultation, inservice sessions on various aspects of the guidelines are offered to the teachers.

The most effective form of inservice sessions, from our point of view, are the ones in which teachers are not talked at by administrators but ones in which teachers can talk with one another and with administrators. Another criterion of effective inservice training is the visible support and actual involvement of at least three groups of administrators: the consultants, the superintendents, and (above all), the principals. The consultant who doesn't have the support and involvement of the superintendent and principal for a new program may as well forget the program. Too frequently, consultants hear teachers say "I know what you are saying is right. But my principal won't let me." Or "How can I do such and such, when my superintendent wants so and so?" Occasionally, these statements are really excuses, but for the most part are valid reasons for not implementing new programs.

One of our recent successful inservice series was on teaching writing for teachers of Grades 1 and 2. The first essential step was the meeting of the consultants and supervisors before the series was advertised. We discussed thoroughly the following topics: What is Ministry of Education policy? Do we have a common interpretation of that policy? Do we agree on method and approaches to teaching writing in primary grades? What is happening now in the primary classrooms of the borough? What improvements do we want to see taking place? How are we going to bring these improvements about? This first step is essential because teachers must hear consultants and superintendents saying the same things.

The second step was easier: Plan a series of four, release time, inservice sessions to be offered between the middle of October and the middle of December.

In the third step, the superintendents called a meeting of all principals of junior schools. At this half day meeting, the superintendents and consultants presented a digest of the series' content. We then asked the principals to explain the series to their Grade 1 and 2 teachers. But there was one important proviso. If the principal did not feel comfortable with what was to be presented and could not offer positive, active support to teachers participating in the series, then the principal should not mention the series to the staff. The principal who could support the concepts was then asked to identify one teacher who *wanted* to take part in the series. Teachers were to attend the series only if they expressed a desire to learn. Principals could attend the series if they wished but would be expected to do everything the teachers did.

Sixty-seven teachers and principals signed up for the release time series. Upon signing, the teachers also agreed to attend four nonrelease time sessions in the winter term.

At the first session, the superintendents and consultants gave a presentation on writing as a learning process, inventive spelling, and ways to get started. Each teacher was to select a few children with whom to work. The teachers were to begin the writing process with those children within the next three school days and bring three or four pieces of one child's writing to the session two weeks later.

A large portion of the subsequent series was devoted to small group discussions of the writing samples, problems, and, in the later sessions, signs of growth and improvement in the writing. The principals also worked with a small group of children on a daily basis. A superintendent who couldn't block time into one school each day tried the program with his sons at home. The consultants visited as many of the classrooms as possible. The teachers, principals, consultants, and superintendents all worked together. There was no "we-they" syndrome.

After the first meeting, a panel of consultants and superintendents answered teachers' questions and discussed their problems at each session. Formal presentations on procedures and methods were kept brief; small group discussions dominated the meetings.

During the winter term, the afterschool sessions were based on subjects which the participants suggested rather than on what the consultants thought necessary. Group discussion and examination of the children's writing continued to be the focal points of the meetings in most cases. Two developments surprised many of the teachers. First, the original small group of children expanded naturally and easily into larger groups as other children became interested and ready to begin the program. Second, many teachers reported that children who wrote almost every day or at least three times a week improved rapidly in reading. Some teachers said children whom they thought would not begin to read until the end of Grade 1 or the beginning of Grade 2 were reading by January.

The consultants noted three effects of the series. One effect was that teachers who had not been in the series asked the consultants to come to their classrooms to show them how to get started. Other teachers virtually demanded that another series be offered. Third, some of the principals who had evinced little enthusiasm when they first heard about the series were now asking for inservice for their school. Word of mouth is the best form of advertising and, if the mouth spreading the word belongs to an administrator, then programs are bound to take off.

When instituting a new program or shifting the emphasis in language arts, four groups of people need educating: the students, the teachers, the principals, and the parents. Just as teachers can do little without positive and active support from the principal, they will encounter great difficulty if they don't quickly secure the understanding and support of parents.

We secure this support in three ways. Meetings of consultants or principals and parents at school are effective. Parents quickly become enthusiastic if they are shown not only what is happening in the classroom but why. "Why" involves brief but dramatic presentations on theory. Parents digest theory rapidly if presentations are brief but effective.

The second way is to send a letter to the parents explaining the language program. A letter, which will get wider coverage but be less effective than meetings, is necessary if the teacher sends samples of students' writing home and has accepted inventive spelling and grammar or usage faults. A brief explanation of why the teacher is carrying out such practices will reassure most parents and will help to avoid parental concerns and complaints. The principal or superintendent should at least approve the letter to the parents, if one of them does not write it with the teacher.

The most effective way to work with parents is to have them visit the classroom and take part in the program, rather than merely observe. If possible, a teacher-parent conference about the program and the student's participation in it should be included, with the emphasis on the program rather than the student.

In order to operate an effective language program, teachers need more materials than many schools can provide. For example, in Etobicoke we have Saint George's Circulating Library. This library is made up of about 50,000 copies of picture books, easy to read books, novels, anthologies of verse, and basal readers. Teachers may borrow single copies, group sets, or class sets for an extended period of time. The flexibility of the library encourages effective programs of varying design and ensures that no teacher is forced to have only one basal reader for a class. The only kinds of materials teachers cannot borrow from the library are workbooks or reading labs.

In too many school districts in North America, a philosophical split exists between curriculum departments and psychology or special education departments. Curriculum departments tend to be developmental in their approach; the psychology or special education departments tend to be behaviouristic. This split confuses teachers because they hear different approaches for helping students with disabilities from two influential departments. In Etobicoke, we are fortunate that the curriculum department and the special education department consistently work together. We help each other write guidelines for teachers, we present inservice sessions together, and we act as a team in advising school staffs on how to modify language and mathematics programs for children with learning disabilities. Our administration makes it quite clear that these modifications must be squarely based on borough guidelines which are, of course, based upon ministry policy. The borough policy is that the program effective for the able child is, with modifications, suitable for the learning disabled child. The teachers see us working together and saying the same things, and they are reassured, encouraged, and helped to provide effective programs for all students.

In summary, the Ontario Ministry of Education develops provincial guidelines. Those guidelines contain policy statements which the classroom teacher must implement. (Of course, no teacher has ever been jailed for not implementing the policy.) The policies are based upon cognitive development and language as process. Implementation of the policies is not expected to take place overnight, but review teams from the ministry visit schools to determine the extent that jurisdictions and teachers are implementing the guidelines and to indicate where improvements should be made.

Local educational administrators are also expected to interpret the ministry policies for the teachers and to help the teachers implement the policies. The administrators are expected to develop local guidelines based upon ministry policy and to help teachers develop effective courses of study. The administrators are also responsible for encouraging and extending the implementation of ministry and local guidelines through inservice training and classroom visitation.

In Etobicoke, the administration has gone beyond ministry expectations by supporting and extending such facilities as the St. George's Circulating Library so that the classroom teacher has more teaching materials than local and provincial grants can provide. The administration also helps develop curriculum by fostering a cooperative effort among superintendents, curriculum departments, special education departments, principals, teachers, and students.

The educational Nirvana is not here, but we are moving toward it. We are doing so by trying, as much as possible, to remove the we-they syndrome. We are happy to work with the ministry and, even though ministry policy in Ontario has the weight of law, we do not feel constrained by that policy. Consultants, teachers, superintendents, principals, students, and parents are trying, as much as possible, to work together to provide effective literacy learning in our schools.

Cultivating Teacher Power

Moira G. McKenzie

T raditionally, British headteachers and staffs are responsible for developing the curriculum within their own schools. It makes good sense for the people who implement and maintain programs to plan them. Schools vary widely, of course, in the amount and quality of thinking they put into this crucial task, but they are not expected to work in isolation. A vast support network provides information and advice. Literacy programs are not developed by outsiders, but by teachers planning, selecting books and materials, and providing experiences that will effectively help children achieve literacy. Thus, British teachers are spared the agony of centrally imposed programs—such as Mastery Learning—which are in opposition to almost everything known about how children learn, particularly how they learn language.

This system, however, is not as haphazard as you might think. At the national level, clear policy is provided along with an organizational network which enables local education authorities to consider and elaborate on such policy. Advisers, head teachers, and teachers carefully examine national policy to understand how it came to be and to plan ways of implementing it. One such way is to provide a program of continuing inservice work for teachers to enable them to develop the knowledge and skills they need. In this chapter, the development, impact and implementation of policy will be discussed. I will draw upon my own administrative experiences as director of a teachers' center established by the Inner London Education Authority (ILEA) to provide inservice work with London primary school teachers in the areas of language and literacy.

Developing National Policy

Educational administration and educational leadership are not separate entities but two dimensions of a single process through which policy is formulated, principles are established, and appropriate conditions for learning are set up. While educational leaders identify needs and point the direction in which educational practice should be going, educational administrators are charged with the task of establishing procedures for implementing change. In Local Education Authorities (LEAs) in Britain, the Chief Education Officer (CEO) is responsible for joining education and politics. The CEO's task is to listen to and advise the elected body through the education committee as to how to translate their educational manifesto into sound educational policies and practice.

How then are policies established? To answer this question, two fairly recent documents which have significantly influenced language and literacy instruction in Britain will be discussed.

In 1974, *A Language for Life,* generally known as The Bullock Report (*30*), was published. This was born out of public anxiety about reading, the voiced fear that standards were falling, and the feeling that progressive methods (promulgated by The Plowden Report, *179*) produced good painters but poor readers! Commissioned by the then Minister of Education, Margaret Thatcher, its scope was widened from reading to language education generally. The Report asserted that "the inquiry is essentially concerned with the development of language in education" (p. xxxv). The committee sought evidence from a wide range of interested parties including university, college and school personnel, politicians, parents, and employers. They interpreted their evidence in the context of recent research in literacy, linguistics, and language.

The enquiry aroused a great deal of interest and talk in educational circles and its report was eagerly awaited. A large part of the report was devoted to reading and the teaching of reading. It declared that reading must be viewed "as part of a child's general language development and not as a discrete skill which can be considered in isolation from it," and that "reading, writing, talking and listening should be treated as a unity." With regard to methods of teaching reading, the report clearly states:

> There is no one method, medium, approach, device or philosophy that holds the key to the process of learning to read. We believe that the knowledge does exist to improve the teaching of reading, but that it does not lie in the triumphant discovery, or the rediscovery of a particular formula....We believe that an improvement in the teaching of reading will not come about from the acceptance of simplistic statements about phonics or any other single aspect of reading, but from a comprehensive study of all the factors at work and the influence that can be exerted upon them. (pp. 77-78)

Sadly, these assertions about reading and language were not much in evidence in Part 3 of the report which dealt specifically with the teaching of reading. The public was assured that reading standards had not fallen (NFER Test NS6),* but that more attention needed to be paid to the changing literacy needs and demands of present day life.

> It is obvious that as society becomes more complex and makes higher demands in awareness and understanding of the members the criteria of literacy will rise. (2.2)

The outcome of this report was a wider understanding of the relationship between language and learning, and language and literacy epitomised by the title given to the report, A Language for Life. After its adoption, Her Majesty's Inspectors (HMI)** and local education authorities (LEA) began making decisions in light of the report's proposals. Conference money enabled advisers and university and college teachers to meet and revise their policies and reshape their programs for both preservice and postgraduate courses. Inservice courses at teachers' centers helped head teachers and school staffs rethink and rewrite language and literacy policies for their own schools. The Bullock Report influenced policy directly and set people to thinking more seriously about the central role of language in education and the relation between language competence and education generally. The summary clearly stated that improved language performance comes through its purposeful use. Once teachers realize the importance of developing language and literacy the problem then becomes one of implementing such practices in classrooms (p. 128).

In 1978, another document, Primary Education in England (182), reported on certain aspects of 7, 9, and 11 year old children's learning in 1,127 classes in 542 schools throughout England and Wales (p. vii). This survey was based on the direct observation of children's work by HMIS experienced in primary education. Their observations involved the whole range of work in the primary curriculum, including language development and reading standards. The report was addressed "to those who carry responsibility at any level for decisions about education" (p. viii). It expressed the hope that:

> Teachers and heads of primary schools, will, together with their local authority and its advisory and specialist services, consider how their work might best be developed in the light of their findings.

---

*National Foundation of Educational Research, developers and publishers of Reading Test NS6 for 11 year olds and Reading Test BO for 9 year olds.
**Her Majesty's Inspectors of Schools—a group of central government officials, who inspect schools, who advise the Department of Educational Policy, and make links between central and local education authorities.

The report confirmed that teachers gave a high priority to the teaching of basic reading skills but added that "graded readers were given too much attention at the expense of other and more profitable forms of reading material" (p. 47). It added that:

> Higher average NFER reading scores for 9 year olds were associated with those classes where children made good use of book collections or libraries. Stories and poems were read to children in a higher proportion of the classes with above average NFER reading scores than in other classes. (p. 96)

It also asserted that "The teaching of skills in isolation, whether in language or mathematics does not produce the best results" (p. 112). And, most significantly in terms of classroom practice, it stated:

> The general educational progress of children and their competence in the basic skills appear to have benefited where they were involved in a programme of work that included arts and crafts, history and geography, music and physical education,and science, as well as language, mathematics, and moral education, although not necessarily as separate items on a timetable. (p. 114)

A clear, considered statement such as this supports and encourages educators generally, and classroom teachers in particular, who live with constant pressures from the vocal "back to basics" groups who focus on the most minimal and simplistic reasons for developing literacy in schools. The report supported the view that language is best learned in use, and that the quality of the learning opportunities directly influences the learner's language development. This applies as much to reading and writing, as it does to spoken language. It also provides insights as to how we approach teaching children from the many different language backgrounds found in our school today.

The Administrator's Responsibility

Administrators come in many shapes and sizes. They range from the top person such as a CEO or superintendent, to inspectors and curriculum advisers, head teachers or principals, and inservice personnel. They constitute a team, each with a clearly defined role, each understanding and fulfilling that role, yet, successfully drawing from and feeding into the whole; thus, building a powerful support system for the schools.

In general, the administrator's responsibility is to promote effective learning for all children. Administrators are often pressured by many special interest groups that seek to provide for the special needs of underprivileged children, for mainstreaming handicapped children, for English as a second language learners, for native language teaching, and for a host of other particular interests. Administrators are the first targets of their political masters, the money suppliers, the back to basics advocates, the cranks, and political point makers. If they are to make wise decisions, to engage in vital educational discussion, administrators must be both up-to-date in educational thinking and in touch with what is going on in the schools. They need to care about education for all children, to know what is possible, to be able to recognize outstanding educational practice, to be aware of ordinary practice, and to be able to identify what is amiss where practice is less than good. They need to understand the value of treating teachers as partners and of enabling them to see themselves as professional thinkers and decision makers. They also need to understand the power and influence teachers wield in the classroom for making life and learning better or worse for the children they work with each day. Excellence in language learning arises fundamentally from the quality of the child's day to day living; current research has made this point overwhelmingly clear. Administrators' major responsibility is to ensure that conditions are right for effective learning.

The problem then arises of implementing policies and disseminating current language learning research in the place where it really matters—the school. Without knowledgeable teachers, classrooms will go on as they have for decades. Curiously, teachers are frequently urged by laypeople and social pundits to teach children in the same way their parents and grandparents were taught. Would there not be consternation if this happened in other professions? How much confidence would these educational reactionaries have in doctors or dentists who were treating their patients with methods from 20 or 30 years ago? Yet money and resources for the continued growth of teachers through inservice education is often speedily cut when belt tightening is the order of the day. Inservice education should be the right of every teacher, with provision made for it in every budget.

Inservice Provisions

Inservice education is needed both inside the school and in specially designed courses and study groups outside school. Most teachers have to make significant changes in their classrooms to implement the results of current research. Many must begin with a change in attitude if they are to apply such information creatively and develop their problem solving skills. Teachers need inservice experiences that will challenge them to think more clearly and deeply about what they are doing and how children learn language. They do not need courses that "service" them with erudite lectures or recipes for instant success. Change does not come about when teachers have things done to them. Reid (*189*) suggested that the best inservice work seems to arise in schools when:

> Teachers are already creating "thinking schools," i.e. schools in which all members of staff participate fully in seeking solutions to those problems which they themselves define as being of the highest priority. (p. 8)

Schools should expect their local support systems to provide knowledgeable help from outsiders. But teachers also need the encouragement and help of their colleagues. Hence, teachers should have opportunities to meet with teachers from other schools, as well as from their own, to share experiences, triumphs, and difficulties.

Teachers also need to become more knowledgeable about research, and other available resources. Additionally, they need help in incorporating such ideas into their thinking and teaching. Teachers' centers play a vital role in providing meeting places for a variety of such learning experiences. These activities also arouse awareness and interest in enrolling in courses available at universities and polytechnics where ideas and knowledge are explored in greater depth, but always in relation to the needs of the schools.

In many areas in Britain, teachers are granted paid leave for one year from their schools to take diploma or MA courses. All such courses include a major work, such as a dissertation or long essay, that involves teachers in action research. Examples of areas recently investigated by teachers include the following.

- Developing of children's concepts of storytelling and writing
- Representation of meanings and children's understanding of their representations
- Reconstruction of meaning from text
- Relationships between mathematical language and mathematics

At the end of these leaves, many teachers return to their schools renewed, ready to take on posts of responsibility, become principals, or perhaps to join the staffs of colleges or teachers' centers. In this way, the thinking school is recharged, and contact is made with current educational research and thinking. It also keeps inservice educators in close touch with teachers and the work they are doing in schools and the problems they meet in their daily lives. Teachers' centers provide a meeting place for this continued interaction.

Teachers' centers are organized to allow teachers to make decisions about how the centers should operate and how to use them. They are staffed by experienced teachers, full or parttime. They are generally multipurpose centers in that they consider the whole school age range and all subject areas. The ILEA provides ten such centers, one in each division, to foster all aspects of the curriculum.

ILEA also maintains specialist centers to serve all the divisions. The Centre for Language in Primary Education (CLPE), which I direct, is a specialist center charged with fostering language and literacy in any of the Authority's 800 primary schools in which the faculty wishes to work with us. The Centre has four fulltime staff members who are experienced in primary education as teachers or principals, and who possess an understanding of language and language learning. A librarian and two advisory teachers on two year secondments are also on the staff.

The Role of CLPE

The Centre is located in Central London, on one floor of an old school building. Part of the staff's responsibility is to set up and maintain a children's library, materials for reading instruction, and teachers' reference books and working manuals. Since each school selects its own books and materials, teachers need the opportunity to examine and discuss them with others. A member of CLPE staff is always available with assistance and advice. The goal is to give children worthwhile reading materials rather than to promote a particular reading scheme. "Teacher-proof" materials are viewed as doing nothing but stunting the teacher's professional growth.

Centre staff work in schools and, when invited to do so, join school staffs in considering certain aspects of their language or reading programs. Courses and study groups are offered in our specialist center, in local centers, and in schools. The range of topics includes children's literature, beginning reading and writing, developing spoken language, extending literacy, developing children's writing, and so on. Our goal is to help teachers understand the nature of language and literacy and to apply this knowledge while working with all children whether they be gifted, slow learners, native speakers, or learning English as a second language. Teachers must deal with this range of abilities and purposes each day in their classrooms.

With the help of the ILEA, the Centre staff published guidelines for language instruction, *Language in the Primary School,* along with a range of video programs related to beginning reading and extending literacy throughout the primary school. Teachers are also made aware of other resources, including video programs from the Centre for Urban Educational Studies (CUES), which presently help teachers understand how to support second language learners in the classroom while they participate in worthwhile learning experiences. Additionally, our regular publications, *Lan-*

guage Matters and *Tried and Tested* (*47*) describe successful classroom practices and are generally written by teachers themselves.

Teachers are constantly encouraged to reflect on and validate their own work with children. From this, the Centre staff gets insights into how teachers think as they begin to identify their own problems. Problem areas often identified by teachers include the following.

- Deprivation—dealing with children with no language
- The multicultural and second language learning aspects of their classes
- Lack of comprehension in reading
- Children's inability to read and write in curriculum areas
- Children's disinclination to write
- The need for grammar instruction, in spoken and written language.

The Centre staff, however, tries to help teachers view their problems within broad areas of knowledge.

- The nature of language
- How language is learned and developed
- Collaboration and interaction between child and child, and child and adult
- The influence of stories on language development
- The reading process
- How children learn to read
- How classroom contexts affect spoken and written language
- Involvement with literature.

The notion that there are children with "no language," or who "speak only in monosyllables," is evaluated in the light of research studies such as Gordon Wells' *Language at School and at Home,* in which transcripts were studied of the same child talking at home and at school. Then, through school based follow up work, teachers collect their own data from their "nonspeaking" children. Two examples offered by teachers follow.

In the first example, teachers read a story to a child (or two or three children), so that the children could see, touch, and talk about the book as parents and children often do at home. Then the teacher invited one child to "read" the story and tape record the reading. The teacher then wrote a brief language profile about the particular child. One teacher described John, aged 5.2, as one with hardly any language and "unable to put together even a simple sentence." The story she read was *The Chick and the Duckling*. Part of the text and John's "reading" are shown below.

Text	John "reading" the text
A Duckling came out of the shell.	A duck came out of a egg.
"I am out!" he said.	"I'm out of my egg," he said.
"Me too," said the Chick.	"So am I," said the Chick.
"I am taking a walk" said the Duckling.	I'm going for a walk," said the Duck.
"Me too," said the Chick.	"I'm going for a walk too," said the Chick.
"I'm digging a hole" said the Duckling.	"I'm digging a hole," said the Duck.
"Me too," said the Chick.	"I'm digging a hole too," said the Chick.

The teacher had to revise her opinion of the child's competence, at least as a sentence maker.

In the second example, the teacher played a tape of a Turkish five year old boy telling the story of the *Three Bears* with great animation, using English in the best way he could. Later on, we heard the same teacher in a question-answer exchange with the child where the child's contribution was limited to long pauses and monosyllabic, uncertain responses.

In this way teachers find hard evidence of how their children use language, with more or less competence in different contexts. By listening to children, and talking with other teachers they can begin understanding that language is always operating within the constraints of a context. Thus, we should not judge children's language competency based on performance in one particular situation. Each child will be more or less competent in relation to the context in which he or she is operating. The task for teachers is to examine the constraints within the school context that reduce or increase children's use of language.

Even when teachers are made more aware of the constraints that operate when they talk with children, they may still have problems changing the teaching practices they have adopted. This was the case with one teacher, who, after listening to and discussing the tape recordings of other teachers interacting with children, became critical of colleagues who required children to guess the answer that was wanted. She went away determined not to fall into the same trap. Despite her good intentions, however, the following is part of a transcript of one or her later lessons.

> Teacher: Yes, I know—yeah I know that you are telling me the names of the birds, but what is it actually doing? It's swooping down—You've told me it's attacking—you've told me it's looking—you've told me it's catching small animals, but what is it actually doing? What kind of creature is it?
>
> Pupil: A bloodthirsty creature?
>
> Teacher: Well—I suppose it is bloodthirsty.
>
> Pupil: Vulture.
>
> Teacher: Look....Remember when we were doing the caves and the cave people? Right? There were some—some of us that were—acting like the ones that went out and caught food—what kinds of characters were these characters that went out and got the food?
>
> Pupil: Hunters.
>
> Teacher: *That's the word I'm looking for. Hunters!* All those creatures—the falcon that you mentioned before, the eagle, the cat, the dog. They're all special kinds of animal—all those animals are hunters. Now why is man—why are people—why do people have their eyes in the fronts of their faces?

Neither language concepts nor how to encourage their development can be easily learned. Knowing some of the problems and their possibilities enables teachers to make a start, but putting their knowledge and theories into action is a long, challenging process. It forces teachers to rethink the very basis of their whole teaching strategy. Yet understanding how to build bridges between children's language and the language used in school is crucial if more children are to be successful school learners. Donaldson (60) raises the question of why so many children find school learning difficult. By reworking some Piagetian tests she demonstrated that more children were successful when questions made sense to them and when they were framed in contexts.

The preceding examples demonstrated how inservice experiences can provide teachers with opportunities to examine their own perceptions of language and literacy, to collaborate with colleagues with specialized knowledge, and to explore particular issues.

The Centre (CPLE) also affords teachers who are responsible for language and literacy development in their schools the chance to publish their thoughts and experiences in the Centre's journal, *Language Matter.* This opportunity encourages teachers to link theoretical issues discussed in the Centre and university courses with their work in school.

The remainder of this chapter gives four examples to illustrate the creative efforts of teachers as they apply and supplement their knowledge of language and literacy learning in their classrooms from day to day.

The first example comes from Sue Powlesland who wrote:

> I was interested in finding out what my children feel about writing because I felt that this would make my teaching more attuned to them and therefore, more effective.

She designed a format using Jessie Reid's "Learning to Think About Reading" (*189*) as a model. She asked ten children (five were 5.6 years, 5 were 6.7 years) the following

- To write something for her
- What they think about their writing
- What the teacher does
- Where ideas for writing come from
- What they know about writing
- If writing really matters

In their responses, the children mentioned cards and letters, shopping lists, checks, crosswords, and "the doctor writes on a bit of paper." They thought the teacher's job was to prevent and correct mistakes. Almost all of them liked writing but they weren't sure where they got their ideas. They all thought it important that they should learn to write. Many of them knew something about the conventions of writing, and had some notion of words, letters, and sentence. The teacher concluded:

> Although they enjoy writing as an activity, they do not see themselves writing for pleasure or for its own sake when they grow up. For younger children, writing is a mysterious self-fulfilling activity, similar to many other activities such as drawing, painting, and junk-modelling.
>
> Talking about their writing is a growing point for children and also a way for the teacher to gain insights into children's attitudes to and understanding of what they are engaged in.

This teacher shared her work with her colleagues and principal. They discussed the children's responses and reexamined the writing demands made upon them.

In the second example, the teacher wrote:

> I felt it would be helpful for us to be able to pinpoint as accurately as we could the stages of children's writing development and to have some idea of the range of writing throughout the school. This would do three things: 1) help us to be more in tune with the progress of individual children; 2) clarify what we meant by writing development; 3) give us the kind of informa-

tion that would enable us to review our efforts to help children tackle writing.

Knowing where and how to start is always a problem. I found it helpful to refer to Marie Clay's outline (46) of writing development. These are the categories as I used them, together with some examples of children's writing. The advantage they offered me was they helped me to organize my impressions of children's development as emergent writers, while focusing on the different strategies they used and also on the kinds of writing they were engaged in.

Teachers collected samples of writing from their children in the nursery class, and from 5, 6, and 7 year olds and grouped them in stages. The second stage, called Tackling Writing, follows.

Strategies children use:

Knowledge of spacing on page.
One to one word correspondence.
Directionality.
Use of known words and letters.

Phonic awareness:

Initial, middle, last sounds.
Punctuation.
Patterning.
Capital and lowercase letters.

Douglas (5 yrs. 7 mths.). Writing a simple sentence using sight vocabulary. One to one word correspondence.

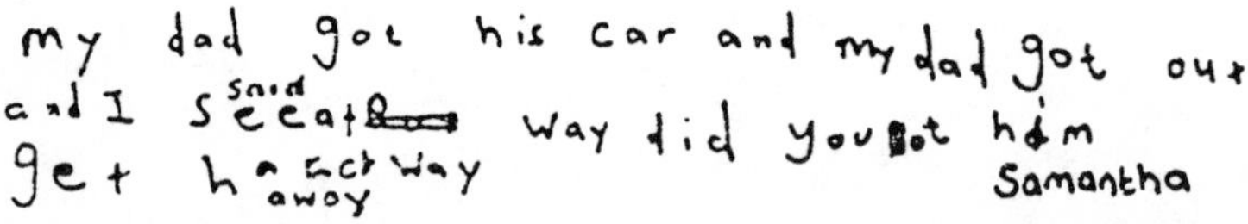

Samantha (6 yrs. 9 mths.). Writing more complex sentences using sight vocabulary and using initial sounds for unknown words. (Accent proves a stumbling block in "away.")

Figure 1. Tackling writing, stage two.

OnE daY I Went to sɕhooL
and at SchooL I SaW A dog
and It waS SaRahS dog and
███████ SaRah and MetteM
SaW the ı dog and TanJa
dog too.

Stacy (5 yrs. 10 mths.). Gaining undertand-
ing of how stories begin and end. Introducing names of people. Using phonics to work
out unknown words. Using full stop. Writing about past experience.

too   haS   The   Went ?
two   had   There   raN   A
to   Rad   They   Mas
       CaT   I   March
       dog   my

home
MuM.
dad.
baby.

Stacy. Good sight vocabulary. Beginning to
see relationship between words.

Miss Ance was on a c'os^(course)
for six weeks and
Miss Ance come and
vflt all the crn^(class)s.
rooms and I
was happy

Daniel (7 yrs. 1 mth.). Sequencing events,
writing about present experience. Talked his
way through writing working out unknown
words with phonics.

a B c d e f g
h i J k l m n
o P q r s
t u v w x
y z bo y dad
girl
home
house
dog

Daniel. Word inventory. Concept of letter
and word. Building up of good sight
vocabulary.

Together the teachers categorized the collection of their children's
writing; they endeavored to identify features within categories and determine what factors influenced particular writing (Figure 2). It was a fine
piece of teacher collaboration.

Fiction	Factual	Functional	Poetry	Language Systems of Other Countries
Use of book language Sequencing of story Starting and finishing story Use of dialogue, names, etc. Title, chapters, index	Relating past and present experience Projecting into future Recording practical work across the curriculum	Can often be used in play situations labels shopping lists menus prescriptions messages recipes animals writing in environment e.g., shops, roads, signs, advertisements	Emphasis on words sounds rhythms rhymes lay-out	Awareness of other forms of writing and their value
Telling and reading good stories gives children a model for their own writing	Good reference books (not many well written for infants) provide a model. If necessary use adult reference books.		A good program of listening to and reading poetry can lead into writing	Having favorite stories translated into other languages and stories from other countries help to encourage children to value other forms

Figure 2. Mapping literacy.

This project was assembled in a large book which Jill Hankey presented as her study at the end of the six week course, and generously allowed us to copy and share with other teachers. Her article concluded:

> I hope these examples show how worthwhile it is to have an overview of at least part of the process of development,...A survey, even on this small scale, helped me and my colleagues to see where we might push ourselves a little harder.

In the third example, David Barton describes a study that originated in his school. He illustrated how CLPE can serve as a medium for sharing good practice. Barton set up displays of children's work at the Centre and talked about it to other teachers enrolled in courses. Barton writes:

This work grew out of a Local Area study which was being done by Upper Juniors. The study had included street surveys and shop surveys, but I was interested to try and discover how far our children recognized some of their cultural roots in the immediate local area. Gerrard Street had its obvious significance for the Chinese community. But what would a Bengali child see, or an Italian or Spanish child? And again what kinds of attitudes would children have to each other's cultural roots? How much did children know about each other's community outside the school?

It was clearly not practical to do this kind of sensitive exploring with the whole class, so I took one child from each of the groups in the class – five in all. Chinese, Bengali, English, Italian and Spanish, (and a camera). At first, the places were very obvious: shops and restaurants, the mosque and the church. But as the walk developed, I became aware of the way in which the children recognized, through their parents, a complex series of cultural roots. "My father goes to play Mah Jong in that flat over there." "We go to a Spanish club down this road." "My father buys his newspapers (Italian) here," and so on. It was a network that stretched across London, embracing mother tongue schools, mosques, and in the case of the Italian community (as with others), informal village associations that link back to Italy itself.

In the newspaper shop we saw the range of languages – greater in range than those used in the school – and I realized that that was the continuing resource available to us. Almost all the children go to mother tongue schools on weekends or in the evenings, but their ability to manage any language other than English is something we continually neglect. It occurred to me that the commentary on our photographs might make some belated recognition of these mother tongue skills. Each boy or girl wrote an English caption on the photographs that most involved them, and then translated that caption into their mother tongue. The photograph and its caption was then passed to someone else to translate into their language, until eventually we had photographs and commentaries in five languages.

What emerged from the process, which was done at a level of seriousness and involvement that one does not often see, was the children's fascination with written language. "Look, 'market' is 'mercado' in Spanish and 'mercato' in Italian!" 'Why are Chinese and Bengali written like that? How do you learn it?" Children were feeling their way into different structures. "In Bengali we don't say it like that, we have to say it a bit different...." It also became clear how much children were aware of language as something that was shared. The writing quickly became a group effort, children supplying to each other the vocabulary and the spelling and the grammatical sense whenever a problem arose.

The report concludes:

It was a small project. And we are lucky to have such an unusually rich environment around us to exploit in this way. But its significance for me lay not in the work that the children produced or in the knowledge I gained of their culture and background, but in the extraordinary ability of all the children to acquire language and retain their knowledge of it. In marked con-

McKenzie

trast to us teachers, who anxiously struggle to 'get them to read and write English,' these children were using writing systems taught them at home, or by unqualified teachers, and recalling language learned in other schools in other countries several years previously. The complex linguistic background of a Bengali child who speaks a dialect of Bengali at home, Arabic at the mosque, and English at school might seem a bar to any effective communication. The ease with which they worked at their task suggested to me how seriously we underestimate children's abilities.

Administrators clearly need to know what is going on in schools, to be able to identify outstanding practice, both for what they can learn themselves about what is possible, and how to share good practice with other

Diana (six yrs.) has an English mother and Italian father and has been educated up to now in Rome. This is her first attempt ever to write in English and she proudly dedicates it to her parents: "*The boy and the girl are having a picnic.*"

Her spelling shows a very thorough understanding of Italian phoneme-grapheme correspondence which she applies with care to the English words she wants to record. What advice should we offer her now?

Figure 3. Emergent writers. The bilingual child.

teachers. So many teachers view multicultural, multilingual classes only in negative terms. It is helpful to share work that demonstrates how other teachers respect and use the rich language learning resources available in their community.

The fourth example comes from teachers enrolled in a six week course designed by Joyce Jurica to help teachers reconsider their school language policies. Policies for teaching language and literacy in schools are not once-and-for-all documents. School staffs find they need to reconsider what is happening in their schools to make appropriate changes. The need to reevaluate literacy policies stems from a variety of happenings such as the reorganization of a school, the appointment of a new head or language post holder, the need to consider new materials and equipment, and teachers' encounter of provocative ideas in their professional reading, or as part of courses they are taking.

Joyce Jurica (47) described the efforts of four teachers who were exploring ways of helping their school staffs reassess their schools' policies for literacy instruction:

> Four teachers collaborated in preparing workshops for their own schools with each teacher preparing a set of notes for her own particular school. They put together taped samples of spoken language, story telling, and reading aloud by children from across the primary age range.
> They were reexamining:
> - the nature of spoken language and its role in the classroom,
> - the nature of reading and the development of children as readers,
> - what is involved in becoming a writer.
> During the course the teachers were engaged in:
> - examining present trends in language research,
> - assessing the current position in their own schools,
> - considering ways of evaluating teaching materials and methods,
> - looking at ways of assessing children's progress,
> - developing relevant programs for use in school.
> One teacher wrote a paper called "Thoughts for Consideration before Formulating a Language Policy." She raised these questions for staffroom discussion.
> - Do we expect children to produce their thoughts in writing without really establishing their ability to interpret ideas orally?
> - Do we instruct our children far more than we actually talk with them?
> - How do we choose books—what do we look for?
> - Do we read a varied range of literature aloud to our children?
> - Do we encourage children to read every word correctly, or do we encourage reading for meaning?
> - Do we think of a reading scheme rather than a reading program?

The teacher concerned reported later that "each section (of the paper) is being used deliberately," "they (the questions raised) have generated a lot of interest and support in the staffroom," "there is a working party engaged in writing a language policy," and finally, "the overall effect is that the school is still working toward a different organization of its language policy." And in doing this, the school continued to look for and receive help from CLPE, and the other support systems offered by ILEA to its teachers.

Teachers also write about the stories they read orally to their classes and how children respond to them. Many such articles are regularly featured in *Tried and Tested,* a periodical published by the Centre. Another Centre publication, *Read Read Read,* was prepared by a working party of teachers to provide information about reading to parents and to suggest ways in which they might help their children. This cooperative effort is another example of teachers and center staff working together for a common purpose.

Teachers' centers are particularly valuable because of their immediate and long term involvement linking schools and vital resources. They are in constant contact with classrooms and schools where imaginative teaching is taking place and also with universities and colleges where intellectual efforts are being made to examine and understand educational processes. Centers are open to teachers on their own terms, bringing to them and taking from them what is theirs. There are no fees to pay, no credits to gain, no increments to accrue, and no papers to write. The ultimate goal is to increase teachers' awareness of what might be, both in classroom terms and in opportunities for further education. Center personnel support groups or individuals who have long term interests they wish to pursue by fostering discussions of ideas, evaluating materials, and sharing experiences. Centers are a valuable resource for teachers whose first interest is to improve their practice and to provide quality educational experiences for the children they teach.

As evidenced in this discussion, many excellent teachers do provide children with language and literacy programs in keeping with current language research. However, the difficulties inherent in extending such ideas and behaviors to a greater number of teachers and schools are considerable. One of the major difficulties is overcoming the stereotypic and outdated presuppositions underlying traditional literacy instruction. Everyone "knows" about reading, and becoming a writer merely requires good handwriting and spelling. Furthermore, many people (including administrators) see art and music, poetry and drama as "frills," which are first to go when money gets tight.

Many authorities also begrudge the idea of "positive discrimination," recommended so cogently in the Plowden Report (*179*). The idea that less privileged children be provided with more books and materials and go on a greater number of school trips is a powerful one. Provisions such as these are mandatory if quality education for *all* children is really our goal. Good firsthand experiences promote effective learning and demand a wide range of language uses as children seek ways of representing their world to themselves and communicating it to others.

Conceptual growth is a collaborative enterprise. It makes its own demands and often takes children into secondary sources for further reading and exploration. Oddly enough, support for providing rich experiences for gifted children is often more evident. They, too, have problems coping within the constrained, stereotypic, unchallenging climate of the classrooms in which they are incarcerated.

Thinking teachers and responsive schools struggle to make headway against the prevailing forces of ignorance and indifference. Administrators are often caught in two ways. First, they have to understand the complexity of teaching if they are to help teachers extend their knowledge and understand better the effects of their own practice. Second, they must understand the limited value of externally mandated directives. Such "help" has little impact, even when supported by relevant research and good materials. Teachers need long term support in defining their own problems, reflecting on and replanning their practices, and sharing their thinking with colleagues and parents. The problem for administrators is to know what kinds of support can best sustain the collaborative efforts within schools, and then to make such support readily available.

Part Five   Role of the Researcher

Overview of the Role

Many teachers seem to have a profound dislike for research findings and theory. At a recent reading conference, a teacher walking out of a general session could hardly wait to "tell the world" about that boring speaker. "All he talked about was 'top to bottom' and 'bottom to top.' " She then enthusiastically praised the previous evening's banquet speaker's humorous presentation.

Why do teachers seem to value research efforts so little? Why do they hold theoretical understandings in such low esteem? In addition to the general lack of descriptive data inherent in quantitative research, many researchers have not provided teachers with an adequate interpretation of their findings. Merely reporting significant/nonsignificant differences does not provide teachers the specific information they need to improve instruction. Reading teachers seemingly need more descriptive input to help them understand more precisely how children apply their previously acquired phonological, grammatical and semantic knowledge to the task of learning to read.

Recent qualitative studies have provided teachers with helpful understandings related to language processing and the nature of the reading process. Smith (206) indicated a need for much more qualitative research when he stated:

> Considerable research remains to be done on how exactly children succeed in learning to read and write, but it will not be done by researchers who believe that such learning is a matter of mastering programmatic reading and writing skills. Instead there is a great need for longitudinal and ethnographic studies of how children come to make sense of print and its uses.

The researcher's role in literacy instruction, then, is to provide teachers with more definitive information regarding the processing of print and of how children acquire this ability. Future reading research should perhaps begin with more realistic assumptions about the nature of language learning and reject the traditional notion that only quantitative research studies can be "rigorous."

In "Theory, Practice, and Research in Literacy Learning," Emans deals with the development and use of theoretical and practical knowledge; he ends with guiding principles for translating research into practice. Henderson, in "Reading Research at the One Century Mark," presents an overview and critical analysis of selected reading research starting with the work of E.B. Huey. Finally, Page discusses the current whole language fragmentation issue in the context of general research concerns.

Even though each author approaches the role of the researcher from a different perspective, all three recommend or imply a guarded stance against exhortation and espousing one particular point of view. This good advice which helps one avoid becoming a part of the "lunatic fringe" (as Page calls it), however, needs to be accompanied with substantive efforts to interpret and disseminate research findings more effectively to those involved with literacy learning.

Theory, Practice, and Research in Literacy Learning

Robert Emans

O ur schools are under attack. Taxpayers are concerned that money allocated to education is not being well spent. Parents are worried that their children are not receiving a quality education. Teachers complain of "burn out" and unreasonable criticism from self-serving and special interest groups. As a result, our schools are increasingly in danger of adopting practices inconsistent with the nature of learning and the type of education citizens of a democratic society need. Something effective must be done and done soon. The resolution of this crisis depends upon the degree of professionalism of the men and women working in education.

Teaching is a profession. As a professional activity it:

> Possesses a body of knowledge and a repertoire of behaviors and skills (professional culture) needed in the practice of the profession; such knowledge, behavior, and skills normally are not possessed by the nonprofessional.
>
> Is based on one or more undergirding disciplines from which it draws basic insights and upon which it builds its own applied knowledge and skills. (*135*, pp. 6-7)

A report prepared recently for the U.S. Department of Education concluded that "the knowledge base for the scientific grounding for teaching is now available and increasing" (*205*, p. vii). The report continued:

> The failure of research to make as great an impact upon practice as it might have done is not to be attributed so much to lack of research knowledge as the fact that pedagogical faculties largely ignore research findings as they train school personnel, especially teachers and administrators. (p. 54)

The sad fact is that the knowledge base of education is often ignored by curriculum developers, college professors, administrators, teachers, and even researchers. In spite of an ever increasing body of professional literature, elaborate information networks, sophisticated statistical techniques, summaries of research, and summaries of summaries, the results of research have had little effect on the quality of schooling in general and on literacy learning in particular. The quality of teacher education is impeding the development of teaching as a profession. Teacher educators seem ignorant of the relationship of knowledge to the design and practice of teaching. Those who prepare and supervise teachers have failed to keep abreast of, and apply advances in, basic knowledge to teacher education and the school curriculum. The proper channeling of knowledge is necessary to prepare teachers to behave professionally. What is needed is an understanding of the nature of knowledge and how that understanding relates to the teaching profession.

The Development of Knowledge

Often when people speak of theory and practice they regard practical knowledge as useful and theoretical knowledge as comparable to idealism, akin to personal philosophy or individual opinion. Actually, there are more precise meanings for theory and practice (*140*). For purposes here, the distinction between these two concepts is that theory relates to generalizations about practice. Whenever we tell someone else how to do something we are using a theory. Practice refers to behaviors and labels related to specific incidents. For example, to say that "adult human beings are between three feet and eight feet tall" is a theoretical statement about human beings. To say that "Joe Smith is five feet ten inches tall" is a practical statement since it is about a specific case.

Generalizations, or theories, have a number of characteristics. For example, they state a relationship: "Adult humans *equal* people who are between three feet and eight feet tall." They predict: "If adult humans are measured, they will be found to be between three feet and eight feet in height." They make claims that may eventually be proved false: "A tribe of Indians in the jungles of Brazil will be discovered that includes adults measuring more than eight feet."

Humans have a natural propensity for forming generalizations to explain past outcomes and predict future ones; they do not need to be taught to do so. Instead, they must learn to delay and control their thought processes (learn not to jump to conclusions) as they go about theorizing to explain events or formulate generalizations. This controlled thought process is a prerequisite of the scientific method and a critical feature of all professional practice. Central to the scientific method of theory building is the hypothesis (literally a half-theory or a half-generalization) which is a tentative theory held in abeyance until enough evidence warrants elevating it to the status of a scientific theory. But since additional evidence may refute a theory, it is never possible to claim with absolute certainty its validity. Thus, in a sense, all theories remain, more or less, hypotheses. To practice, though, we must behave as though a certain hypothesis is valid, and thus a theory, until new evidence challenges it.

In unscientific thought, theories are no different in nature from scientific thought except that they are supported only by evidence that has not been gathered through controlled procedures. Hypotheses unchecked by objective evidence are no more than superstitions and unfounded personal opinion. Whenever humans learn from experience—that is, when they improve their practice—they have knowledge. When they can tell someone else how to improve their practice they have a higher level of knowledge. Every effort should be made to make the hypotheses used in education as scientific as possible, i.e., based on objective evidence.

All validated theory, or knowledge, has its historical roots in human occupations, e.g., growing food, building things, decorating objects, keeping evil away, maintaining records, and communicating ideas. As Dewey (55) once said:

> In the history of the race the sciences grew gradually out from useful social occupations. The occupations of a household, agriculture, and manufacturing as well as transportation, and intercourse are instinct with applied sciences. (pp. 235, 321)

As knowledge has become better organized and more useful for making predictions, professions have developed in areas such as agriculture, engineering, medicine, and teaching. As our common knowledge becomes further removed from the level of direct events, i.e., from basic occupations and the professions, by being symbolized and taught, the more it can be generally used: abstracted theory, through logical extensions, begets theory. Theories that are generally demonstrated to be valid are organized into a framework which is referred to as "formal knowledge," and are developed into academic disciplines, e.g., history, chemistry, and mathematics. The frameworks for every subject area are incomplete, and would be even more so, except that they are supplemented by hypotheses made from logical extensions. This is also true of educational theory.

Some examples of the roots and current sources of information on academic disciplines are: chemistry from textile manufacturing, agriculture, and fishing; physics from engineering; biology from agriculture, fishing, and medicine; and psychology from teaching, business management, and government. In turn, newly formed academic disciplines have proven to be of help to the professions; for example, sociology, anthropology, and psychology provide considerable guidance to the teaching profession. Thus, a cycle is created: from basic occupations (professions) to academic discipline back to professions. As was noted previously, those academic disciplines having specific significance to a profession become what is generally thought of as the "supporting disciplines" for that particular profession—physics for engineering, psychology and sociology for education, and so forth. Although a basic discipline may be "pure" inasmuch as an immediate use for it may not be obvious, if it never has a use to anyone it will eventually lose its significance and fade away, alchemistry and astrology for example.

Theoretical and Practical Knowledge

Teaching, since it is a profession, is concerned with the use of knowledge, not the development of knowledge for its own sake. Thus, the nature of the relationships between theoretical and practical knowledge is of special concern. Theoretical knowledge leads to conclusions about the likely effects of actions; the result of an experiment or a generalization from personal life for example, but it does not and should not be translated directly into action in the classroom. It must be compromised in the light of overall practices. In contrast, practical knowledge is the outcome of the compromising process and gives rise to professional practices or actions in the real world of the classroom. Thus, it is important to consider the differences between theoretical and practical knowledge, taking into account the advantages and disadvantages as well as the uses and misuses of each.

The use of theory, particularly as it relates to education, has its limitations, as Schwab (201) has said,

> The curriculum field is based upon an unexamined reliance on theory in an area where theory is partly inappropriate in the first place and where the theories extant, even where appropriate, are inadequate. (p. 1)

Any particular theory may be true, but only because it has left much unsaid. What a theory does not say may be more important than what it says.

> All theories...necessarily neglect some aspects and facets of the case....It abstracts a general or ideal case. It leaves behind the nonuniformities, the particularities....It often leaves out of consideration conspicuous facts of all cases. (p. 11)

For example, physics studies the nature of falling bodies in a vacuum, a condition that does not exist in the real world. A theory that ten year old children like to read about dogs, although valid, not only fails to take into account that Mary (a particular child) prefers to read about horses (a practical statement), but that children in general prefer more to read about other children than they do about animals.

Furthermore, any particular theory can attend to only a very small fraction of the world. Theories can be developed about many aspects of the world which are often unrelated to one another. Theory about the content of what children are interested in reading is unconnected to theory about how children behave in a rote learning task. To complicate the situation even further, especially in the behavioral sciences, theories are often competing. For example, Hodges (*129*) has demonstrated that spelling is taught differently depending upon which of several learning theories the teacher accepts.

Educational theory involves new notions about the nature of children, society, and subject matter. Thus, advances in educational theory gravitate toward the novel. As a result, the effect of theory on practice in schools is often to encourage a swing from one extreme to another, to replace one practice by another, thus forfeiting a steady accumulative improvement. Theory does not often take into account the effectiveness of current practices. As Chall (*38*) has said in respect to reading instruction:

> A new method is rarely completely innovative....Who is to say that retention of some of the old way of doing things is not a crucial factor in improved results? Although the innovations may be critical of the prevailing methods and materials, they incorporate much of the old into the new. (pp. 282-283)

Any change in educational practices must contend with institutions as they exist. Schools and their curricula cannot be dismantled and replaced, but must be changed piecemeal.

Theory often ignores unintentional side effects, which often reflect concerns more important than the issues the particular theory addresses. For example, one early basal reading series was written for urban children and focused on settings in the city, but ignored the general nature of children (*77*). Researchers in education must consider a total setting, not just the aspect under investigation. Improvement in one area of schooling, achievement in reading, for example, may be at the expense of other areas, such as art and music.

Durkin surprised the reading establishment when she found that "many of the procedures likely to improve comprehension and that are mentioned in all the reading methodology textbooks....were never seen." That is, teachers did not use the procedures in the classroom (*68*). It is dangerous to conclude that teaching for higher level comprehension skills should be avoided and replaced by instruction in literal comprehension skills (*195*) just because few teachers currently equipped to teach for anything other than literal meaning (*29, 68, 108*).

Theory is restrictive in another respect. Its purpose is to show that something is right or wrong, and so it reduces the number of alternative courses of action. On the other hand, in real life situations, which are uncontrolled and complex, the concern is usually to select the best action for a particular situation from a number of good alternatives. In practice, one is eager to expand the number of good options and not to limit them as theory is likely to do. Researchers should be concerned with identifying as many good procedures for teaching as possible. Instead, researchers today have focused their attention on showing that a given procedure is best under all circumstances, usually from a particular theoretical perspective.

As Petty and Jensen (*171*) have said:

> Analyses of language structure are based on widely different theories (structural and transformational-generative are the best known). The theoretical differences lead to differences in definition, terminology, and procedures. (p. 27)

They go on to quote Paul L. Gavin as saying:

> The linguistic tail should not try to wag the educational dog. That is, linguists—as well as other devotees of linguistics—should be aware of the fact that linguistic factors are only one of the many considerations that have to be taken into account in the educational process. Needless to say, psychological, sociological, and just plain human factors, not to mention economic and political considerations, play a significant role in education. In this broader context the linguistic variables turn out to be important, but not necessarily primary. (p. 47)

Research for Education

It would be incorrect to conclude that academic theory or research in education has no use. Distinctions for the application of research within schools can be made along a sequence of adaptations from the state of pure research, through applied and action research, and finally to evaluation. In pure research, hypotheses are tested in relation to firmly established theories from the basic disciplines; the theory developed relates back to the basic discipline. Applied research generally extends the theories of pure research from the basic disciplines into the professions; hypotheses about biology are extended into medicine, for example. In the case of educational theory, generalizations are formed about specific dependable outcomes of repeated practices. Action research takes the hypotheses of the applied research of the professions and tests their effects in a variety of specific practical settings. Evaluation translates the theories of action research into norms (repeated outcomes of specific practices) and uses the norms as standards for determining the success or failure of these practices in a particular classroom setting.

In the pure research of many academic disciplines, researchers can often conduct laboratory experiments in which variables are artificially controlled, held constant, manipulated, as well as treated statistically. In contrast, in action research in specific settings, the researcher must use intact groups and so can study only through statistical devices. Case studies, as a further extension, can be useful in research at the cutting edge of a line of inquiry where hypotheses are first formed and, interestingly enough, at the other end of the continuum, in evaluation, where the results of inquiry can describe the effects on individuals of theories tried out in actual practice.

It is inappropriate for researchers in teacher education, referred to here as action and applied researchers, to be engaged in what is commonly thought of as pure research, research that advances knowledge for its own sake, as in linguistics, psychology, sociology, or anthropology. It is best to leave such research to the specialists in the various basic disciplines. When teacher educators have attempted to conduct pure research, their results seldom contribute much to either the basic disciplines or to the teaching profession. Instead, teacher educators should focus, as do other educators and administrators, on applied and action research and on evaluation. A word of caution, however, should be made about applied and action research. Green and Petty (*105*) stated:

> Experiments must be carefully designed and controlled, however, since massive try-outs and action research tend to be inconclusive, often resulting only in opinion—usually reflecting the initial bias of the "experimenter." (p. 21)

Some Guiding Principles

Teachers must benefit from scientific research translated into terms of their practice. They must be kept informed of the results of their own practice and those of their peers in comparable settings. They must differentiate between practices based on educational theory and those that are parochial or subjective. Only then can teachers contribute to the development of their profession and be professional themselves. Research in education should follow, as far as possible, the principles established for pure research. Some of these principles follow.

1. *Theory should be based on objective evidence, where possible, rather than on personal opinion.* Research to support educational theory should: state problems clearly with well defined terms; use representative samples and reliable and valid instruments in collecting data; analyze data properly, using, when appropriate, statistical devices; and draw only those conclusions supported by the evidence gathered.

2. *Research problems in education should be approached from as many theoretical positions as possible.* Education is concerned with individuals, groups, culture, communication, and subject matter. Almost any decision in education must, to be sound, take into account many aspects of the real world. As one author has put it:

> No curriculum grounded in but one of these subjects can possibly be adequate, defensible,...[It] can be nothing but incomplete and doctrinaire....A single theory will necessarily interpret its data in the light of its one set of principles, assigning to these data only one set of significances and establishing among them only one set of relationships. (pp. 8, 13)

For example, some people have asserted that the failures of modern mathematics and science curricula have been due to a narrow focus on subject matter without adequate concern for the nature of children and society. Other people have accused teacher education of being preoccupied with the area of educational psychology.

> Once we specialize or channel our knowledge generation through one discipline we have limited our potential for understanding....Most people believe that if they study psychology they will understand themselves and others....Examining the work of psychological theorists will reveal how their way of knowing hinders as well as deepens our understanding of human behavior....As a result, when we complain about the inadequacies of teacher education we are, in effect, complaining about the inadequacies of the constructs in educational psychology. (*109*, pp. 8-16)

3. *Research in education should reflect a broad spectrum of classrooms and schools.* Contrary to an often repeated assertion, most college professors are familiar with what goes on in schools. As a study by Yarger and Joyce (*242*) concluded:

> In many quarters, it is assumed that education faculty are somehow in-experienced in teaching. This is manifestly untrue. Faculty in schools and colleges of education have, on the whole, taught for several years. They know the world of schools. (p. 21)

Nevertheless, professors often seem to lose the broad perspective they normally have on education when they conduct research. Of course, consistent with the above principle that research should be based upon objective evidence, research in education must control extraneous variables. By doing so, however, researchers at times seem to lose sight of concerns that are as important as the ones they are studying. Some years ago I studied the effectiveness of emphasizing a reading skills program in a high school English course for underachievers. With respect to that particular program, I found the students could make substantial improvement in their abilities to read without a consequent loss in other areas of the English course of study, but they developed negative attitudes toward reading and schooling (76). What may be gained in respect to a particular objective can be lost in respect to other, perhaps even more important, concerns.

4. *Changes in practice as a result of research findings should be made systematically and cautiously.* Bandwagons in education are far too common. Innovation for the sake of change seems to be the order of the day. As a result, sustained improvement in educational practices is often lacking. The new should be built upon the best of the past. Researchers naturally want the outcomes of their efforts to be recognized and to have an impact on schooling, but they should be modest in interpreting the implications of their research. Otherwise, much of the benefits that can accrue from research may be lost. In some ways, the best of research can, and probably should, have a conserving effect. As Edwards (70) has said in respect to research on the language differences of children:

> Perhaps the greatest contributions of sociolinguists has been the advances from knowledge to ignorance—to a realization that we do not know what we thought we knew in the late 1960's because children's communicative repertoires are not so easily or rigidly characterized. (p. 518)

5. *Current educational research should be well grounded upon the cumulative knowledge base of the past.* Our accumulated knowledge about literacy learning, no doubt, is incomplete and, in certain regards, may be wrong. Nevertheless, researchers must become familiar with earlier research. For example, one investigator claimed that his study on func-

tional literacy was "the first major attempt to describe the reading habits and activities of adults" (*82*, p. 55). In fact, numerous studies on adult literacy have spanned a period of more than forty years. Similarly, much of the current research conducted on vocabulary ignores the work of previous investigators. I have found sixteen recent studies in reading that are comparable to, but do not take into account, similar past studies (*75*).

Many of the controversial issues in education should not be, since much information is available about them. Much of what is known is never implemented and, thus, little progress is being made in improving our schools. Of course, in a democracy, all points of view must and should be heard. But a democracy is also dependent upon communication among specialists and professional practitioners. In respect to schooling, there is much ignorance — even among those who earn their living in this endeavor. Somehow this state of affairs must change if our schools and society are to survive. Researchers in education must take the responsibility of conducting the types of studies that will make a difference in education.

Reading Research at the One Century Mark

Edmund H. Henderson

R esearch in reading has accomplished much in its first hundred years. We know a great deal more about the process than we did, and we are beginning to see, at least in rough outline, the dimensions of those hidden mechanisms which underlie this complex human behavior. Some of our more troublesome pedagogical disputes may soon be resolved, leading to a stronger and more concerted effort by serious educators.

To achieve such a state of concurrence will not be easy, for people love dispute and they indulge this love most freely when uncertainty prevails. Reading, unfortunately, is still a mystery: The tools of science cannot penetrate its mechanisms to the core. Science, nonetheless, can and has defined a limit to our ignorance that does deny educators a license for magic. No longer does anything go. Scientific knowledge has provided definite boundaries for the legitimate exercise of teacherly imagination.

Educators, accordingly, need to recognize and respect this field of operation and develop the strength of character to accept what is yet unexplained with honesty and composure. A first step in the exercise of this judgment must be to recognize that teaching, like husbandry, is an ancient art whose successes and failures have always been shaped by natural conditions.

The traditions of teaching, however, also have empirical roots. A second step then must be to understand that science cannot prescribe teaching. No formula can be written or plan designed to bypass the interplay of mind and mind.

A third step must be to recognize reading as a natural human event, and written language as a social artifact. The written word is a tool of incredible power and one that has been jealously guarded by societies throughout history. Scientists may study reading and educators nurture and exercise its use, but neither scientist nor educator may influence directly those conditions in which, by social blunder or intent, the artifact is withheld or its use restricted.

In 1908, when Huey (*137*) summarized the status of reading research, he described conditions similar to those of today. Studies of text perception at that time showed that the mind could grasp more than the eye could "see." Faced with this anomaly, Huey elected to define the reading process metaphorically. He said that reading was a projection outward from the mind like a lantern slide in which mind served both as light and screen (p. 106). Huey distinguished clearly, however, between this metaphorical description and the empirical formulations which he believed should guide scientific inquiry. He expected that science would work "toward the light" (p. 102) by employing disciplined principles not fanciful descriptions.

Huey's metaphor was a convenient device for describing a scientifically delimited field in which reading instruction must take place. In effect he defined reading as a competence which required the active use of the human mind. Thereafter his pedagogical ideas were philosophically based. Science delimited, but philosophy and commonsense judgment directed, his teacherly opinion.

The limits that Huey declared have not been removed, but progress has been made. The boundaries have yielded a fraction here and there and sufficiently so to clarify some difficult teaching questions. Major advancements have been made in our knowledge of brain physiology and certain aspects of its function. Our technological skills for the measurement of eye movements and exposure time are enormously more refined than they were in 1908. Progress has been made in describing in scientifically adequate ways both language development and the developmental knowledge of written word. Finally, interest has broadened remarkably in language history (*87, 148*) and in the social and anthropological aspects of literacy (*35, 223, 224*).

The crucial question for reading research has always been, "How does the brain do it?" Few laypeople are able to judge the status of research in brain physiology, yet most do know that the complexities are vast and that no final answers are at hand. The work of Penfield and Roberts (*170*), Hebb, (*121*), Prebram (*181*), Geschwind (*88*), and Lenneberg (*150*) comes readily to mind as research which has focused upon language specifically, and upon reading by extension. In my judgment, the most acceptable model of reading to come from this discipline is that of Eric Brown (*28*) who has the unusual qualifications of extended formal study in three disciplines: reading, linguistics, and neurology. His contribution is an information map tracing the time relationships among those central functions called on during a single fixation by a normal reader addressing ordinary text. Brown's statement is conservative and carefully documented; I believe that it must stand as a working reference for any nonmetaphorical assertions about human reading competence.

Brown's model shows that at a moment of fixation the full brain is involved, that there are delimiting temporal events, that these are governed by wonderfully complex motor plans and enjoy an amazing degree of flexibility in execution. The entire sequence works "automatically" and without benefit of conscious direction. This work demonstrates beyond question that the brain is empirically different from a lantern slide or a computer. Brown's model is useful to the educator precisely because it warns against the contemplation of reading as a conscious act or an act that may be programed by conscious design.

Over the past twenty years scientists have carried out a very large number of eye movement studies similar to those undertaken by Huey and his contemporaries. Students of reading are likely to be familiar with the review of this line of research by Wildman and Kling (240). The technical elegance of the machinery employed is astonishing. Even more astonishing, perhaps, is to learn that these tools still lack the power of perfect registry with central function. In the main, findings support those of earlier years, but they do not support the loose interpretation that Huey's metaphor might suggest. There is no evidence that anticipation "feeds" a given percept.

> Any theory that supposes that the reader obtains visual information from and semantically interprets a large area of text (a phrase, sentence, or line at a time) during a single fixation is probably out of harmony with reality (155, p. 85)

Information pick-up at a moment of fixation appears to work fully responding to what is there, not what is "thought" to be there.

Similarly, high precision research using tachistoscopic presentations with extremely fine control of speed and light has been applied to word and letter identification (153 for example). The aim of this work is to sort out the characteristics of those mechanisms thought to underlie text identification. Educators have sometimes acted as if they believed that words were stored in the head like little pictures, though most do know that it could not be as simple as that. Studies of verbal learning suggest that word knowledge is a complex "amalgam" (72) of visual information and phonological, syntactic, semantic and orthographic knowledge. This line of study is related to that carried out in speech perception at the Haskin Laboratory (148). The latter research has found, for example, that phoneme identification is a complex constructive process that a listener exercises automatically in reference to his or her own plan for articulation. Substantive researchers are now exploring the marriage of functions as intricate as these in the act of text perception.

Despite the formidable advancement of technology, precise and perfect measurements of the mechanisms of reading still elude the engineer's grasp. Nonetheless, what has been shown is certainly informative. These works cast out such notions that there are simple modality differences or simple bonds between letter and phoneme or word and spoken word. These findings place an absolute limit upon the education field. No teacher, and of course no scientist, can tell a child how to learn to read. What children do and have been doing for some 2,500 years may provide some guidance, and developmental research may sharpen this commonsense perspective. Ultimately, however, the learner acquires literacy; it cannot be constructed by the teacher.

Developmental research differs from those psychological efforts which focus on finer and finer descriptions of basic mechanisms. Developmental researchers examine large and relatively natural samples of behavior and attempt to find commonalities and progressions which characterize the changing conceptual view of children. Such a clinical method, as Piaget termed it, has a natural attraction for educators who do their work in natural settings and are constantly confronted with the ways of young children as well as what they are learning. Developmental research has, however, a contribution to make to more substantive studies as well (*13*, for example), particularly in reading, which we presently know only as a delimited competence.

To the degree that we are able to describe what children know about words at successive stages, such schemes provide a fruitful testing ground against which to measure the hypothesized mechanisms which must underlie such knowledge. Over the past twenty years a good deal of work has been accomplished in the developmental study of word knowledge (*124, 184*). It has been shown, for example, that when beginning readers know what a word is, they can construct other words by matching letter names to phonemes. They will spell *cape* "kap" and *bit* "bet." This linear match of letter to sound is a robust phenomenon—it is largely independent of instruction and it is found for children learning other alphabetic languages. Only later do children begin to show in their invented spellings a tacit knowledge of vowel patterns. Then *bit* will appear either correctly spelled or possibly as "bite," while *cape* might be spelled "caip." This transition is clearly progressive: It follows the letter-name stage and precedes the correct spelling of syllable junctures in English (*199*).

One inference drawn from this work is that what children do as spellers may reflect in part what they know and use in word identification. Eye movement studies, for example, have long shown beginning readers making a number of fixations per word as if parsing the word letter by letter. In a recent study, letter-name spellers, i.e., beginning readers, did not recall the silent letters in words like *gate* and *sail*, whereas those who spelled by pattern recalled a silent marking vowel more stably than they do a sounded letter (*10, 11, 72*). This concurrence between developmental findings and those derived from research of more formal design is encouraging, and it suggests a natural connection between such research and educational practice.

Certainly there has been no more furious battleground in reading pedagogy than that over whole word versus phonics instruction. The present state of reading research suggests a resolution to that disagreement. Children do achieve developmentally a concept of word as a bound figure that begins and ends. Children do appreciate the sequential relationship of letters to sounds that plays across each word. These understandings are not confined to the surface of the page nor are they consciously held. They are registered and exercised within. Efforts to determine which comes first — knowledge of word or letter-sound matching — are interesting, but probably futile and certainly unnecessary. What is shown is that *both* occur and *both* are relevant. As readers advance in skill, they do not discard this initial "amalgam," but differentiate it more complexly. For children who have passed the letter-name stage, the vowel nucleus and a pattern of letters within the word function as a unit. Thus, a subset of whole *and* part is achieved. This phenomenon is shown both developmentally (*16*) and in formal verbal learning research (*157, 214*).

Doubtless the two most celebrated methods for remedial reading instruction are those of Grace Fernald (*81*) and Anna Gillingham (*89*). The former leans toward whole word instruction, the latter toward isolated phonics. Students of reading should set these works side by side and study them again in the light of contemporary research. Both are elegant techniques in terms of the most discriminating clinical standards. In each plan the teacherly art overwhelms and diminishes any fault or bias, moreover, both approaches do in fact touch the elemental bases necessary to bridge a shaken learner into reading. Neither is just whole word or just phonics regardless of what their authors may have believed. In each plan the learner is constrained to orchestrate both whole and part.

Most children appear to accomplish this intricate temporal synchrony of visual display and language with less formal support and regimentation. Even so, no method of instruction will survive if it does not provide for the integration of text, word, letter, sound, and meaning. Historically those methods that have failed have been those in which one element of the competence has been isolated at the expense of the rest.

In the ancient alphabet method, which survived for approximately two thousand years, children were first taught their letters and then shown brief texts, usually a familiar prayer. They were then told to name each letter and say each word in order. It would be difficult to find a method closer to what children actually do developmentally as they begin to learn to read.

In 1756 Hoole (*132*) noted that some children did not learn letters after a year of drill even though they were beaten for "lack of heed." He guessed these "less ripe witted children" would have advanced more cheerfully, though later, had the beatings been withheld. His hunch was a sound one, for letters alone or sounds alone or whole words alone or even texts alone are insufficient. All the above are required and always as the child can combine them, for we cannot build within the child's brain. An examination of the most successful methods of instruction will show a similar conformity to the basic operations of developing learners. Conversely, an examination of those methods which have been shortlived will show a want of balance; they have been either all phonics, no text or all text, no phonics. Substantive research begins to show why these radical attempts should fail.

Huey's response to the status of reading research was excellent in its day. Certainly he was correct to delimit reading as a competence. His shortcoming was to suppose too ready a solution to his "miracle" (p. 6) and to cast aside the traditions of instruction too freely. He spoke of teaching in the past as a "grab bag of absurd practices" (p. 9) which, presumably, the new science of psychology would soon mend. It has not done so. Unfortunately, the shortcoming of educational practice for the ensuing seventy-five years is that it became a grab bag of absurd scientific applications. Today a sharp reverse of this trend will certainly be required.

The list of our errors is a long one—our misuse of tests, our silly belief in methodological comparisons, our distortion of texts, and our doll baby programs of phonics. These are perhaps our most notorious blunders. Others are less obvious.

Since the early sixties the work of behavioral psychologists has been much denigrated. Chomsky's attack (*41*) upon B.F. Skinner's attempt to describe language in behavioral terms signaled the end of the vaunted stimulus and response. Was this work altogether wrong? Do children not learn certain words by rote? Is habit formation a fiction? Certainly it is not.

Reading teachers today would be well served to review this literature and to review their teaching techniques closely in its light. But is word knowledge more than a habit? Of course it is, and therein lies the fault of misapplication. To design a curriculum of word acquisition on a model of habit strength alone was simply unjustified.

Consider next Leonard Bloomfield's contribution to reading instruction. A brilliant linguist, Bloomfield (22) brought to bear upon reading instruction the full power of his operational analysis of word structure. His word was and is sound, but it sprang from a single model in which, for convenience, meaning was totally neglected. His position was that of the strict behaviorist. Reading programs were built on the Bloomfield model in which pupils were conditioned to respond to limited sets of structurally "regular" syllables. Text was distorted to nonsense and the meaning base for orthography — a fundamental component of Modern English (26, 123) — was totally omitted. That such programs were advertised as "scientifically proven" is a further commentary upon an age of technological credulity.

The radical shift to cognitive psychological models did not stem the tide of absurd borrowings. As thinking and structural models of thought became fashionable, these too were adapted to formal plans for the teaching of comprehension, as if intelligence were a thing that is taught rather than exercised in the act of reading. In the early seventies a reading program emerged in which the study of words was compressed to the vanishing point and text alone was emphasized as the medium of instruction. That this work failed quickly is not surprising, but neither is it satisfactory, for the quality of the writing in the work was an improvement over that of "Dick and Jane." A needed reform was thus dashed on the rocks of extremism.

Today many reading experts who deplore the distortion of text for the purpose of teaching vocabulary by frequency and pattern appear unabashed by the prospect of teaching reading by the guess procedure of the cloze test or by the application of rational schemata to "prime" the reader's mind or to produce readable material by formula. Here as before the competence of the reader and writer is disregarded and the things learners try to do are overlooked. This is not a question of bad science but of faulty application.

Behavioral scientists were starkly neglectful of issues involving understanding in the broader sense. What could be controlled and measured was their universe. The prescriptive application of conditioning principles to reading books led to products that were totally unreal: "Oh Sally look and see Dan fan a man." On the other hand, the associative theory studied by the behaviorists did represent a physiologically valid, albeit limited, aspect of human learning. Most cognitive models in contrast have a far less convincing empirical base. As one examines some of the flow charts depicting the route of information from mind to text and back to mind again, the temptation is strong to add a label saying "Warning: This model may be a metaphor!" Huey was careful to keep the distinction clear.

For the past several decades it has been acceptable to laugh at the behaviorist's view. As the joke goes, "Mr. Skinner can teach pigeons to play tennis, but not to keep score." However, many who perceive clearly the limits of conditioning seem not to see the folly of applying a computer model to human language function. To be sure engineers have programed computers to "read." Computers do so very poorly and without comprehension, yet the achievement is praiseworthy. What does not follow from such work, however, is the notion that similar procedures would be appropriate for human beings. No responsible educator should adopt a program of instruction designed to teach parrots to speak or computers to read.

Huey distrusted the trial and error methods of practicing teachers, and he warned against the influence of publishers whom he felt to be agents of conformity to outmoded practices. Curiously, the major publishers of reading material have tempered the excesses of scientific prescription over the past hundred years. New "Breakthrough Programs" have been produced, but each has quickly faded. The standard and conservative basal, for all of its manifold shortcomings, has remained. The law of the marketplace has constrained the major publishers to the production of materials and plans that teachers find convenient and effective for their children. Doubtless it will seem heresy to many to suggest that teachers in general are better judges of instructional plans than are scientists, but that indeed is my conclusion.

In 1890 James (*139*) warned teachers as follows:

> I say moreover that you make great, a very great mistake, if you think that psychology, being the science of the mind's law, is something from which you can deduce definite programmes and schemes and methods of instruction for immediate schoolroom use. Psychology is a science, and teaching is an art; and sciences never generate arts directly out of themselves. An intermediary inventive mind must make the application, by using its originality. (p. 23)

Obviously, we have not heeded this sound advice. The science of psychology certainly does have its place, and so, of course, do all other areas of research—medicine, neurology, sociology, and linguistics. None, however, may substitute for or directly prescribe the educator's work. What is needed is not less research but more, and this basic work must be accomplished by dedicated scientists in their respective fields. There is a role for educational research as well, but this work must grow from and flow to educational concerns directly.

Some fifteen years ago a convergence model was adopted to review the corpus of reading research and determine a focus for future study. Able scholars from a variety of disciplines participated in this project and useful reviews were achieved in a number of areas (*8, 78* for example). Certainly this work did stimulate both more and better research efforts in the years that have followed. The ill conceived and impossible to interpret methodological comparison studies, the bulk of reading research in the forties and fifties, have all but disappeared from the current literature. A new and much needed interest has developed in the sociocultural factors influencing literacy, an area heretofore almost entirely neglected. Gray and Roger's *Maturity in Reading (104)* is a notable exception. Despite these useful gains, the overall effect of this convergent effort has been disappointing.

The difficulty lies in the fact that reading is not a single specific problem like a disease. To be sure there is such a thing as dyslexia — an inability to learn to read early, or possibly at all, stemming from some malfunctioning of the central nervous system. Research in this area is needed and is being done, but the field is far too complex to yield to sudden urging. There is not the slightest possibility of our achieving a comprehensive mastery of brain language function in the immediate or even distant future. Over and above dyslexia, reading is a normal human phenomenon which has answered remarkably well to the ministration of teachers over the centuries. To suppose that some psychological discovery could change the manner in which reading is learned is simply unreasonable. No theory of learning or conceptual model of intelligence can possibly change the order of things that a child must do to become a fluent reader. There are no easy answers, breakthrough methods, tricks, nostrums, or quick cures for social neglect. Indeed, our repeated attempts in so many of our teaching efforts have led to inconsistency, false hope, and ill temper.

Teachers were the missing ingredient in the convergence research of the late sixties. Researchers are simply unqualified to interpret their work educationally. Teachers do indeed need to know the state of scientific knowledge, just as travelers may need to know that the earth is spherical rather than flat, but they do not need to know the fine points of astrophysics or linguistics or neurology. They need to know about these matters, and they need to feel out the usefulness of such knowledge in the business of teaching. Interpretation at this level requires competence in the teaching art and disciplined scholarship in the study of many diverse disciplines. Such an effort might even yield a useful point of scientific interest, but its true product and its goal must always be better informed teaching.

In raising these criticisms about the application of scientific inquiry to instruction, I have no wish to demean the efforts which have been so painstakingly, sincerely and often brilliantly carried out by young scholars. Let me offer an early work of my own as a negative example (*122*). The topic had to do with reader purpose. The question asked was this: Would well formulated predictions of story outcomes characterize the competence of high versus low achievers on tests of comprehension when intelligence was controlled? Findings supported an affirmative answer.

The difficulty with a study of this kind is that the issue was never in doubt. Worse, it was wrong to submit so important a pedagogical truth to the hazards of statistical analysis and the cumbersome formalities of research design. The findings lent nothing to a theoretical formulation of the reading process and they added nothing that was not already far more adequately described in pedagogy (*137, 215, 216*, for example). Contrast my effort with the far more interesting work of Applebee (*7*) in which the developing concept of "wolf" is traced as a literary symbol. The first work was a waste of time; Applebee's is fascinating and useful to a teacher.

Unfortunately a great deal of what has been called educational research has not stemmed from informed educational questions. Many of our brightest and ablest teachers have deserted their trade before mastering it. They have become quasiscientists and their bent has been to produce "answers" from the theoretical model in vogue. A true scientist does not produce answers for educators; he or she would be horrified by the very thought of trying to do so.

The role of the educator is to know the business of teaching intimately, thoroughly, masterfully, quite as the musician plays and the painter paints. Only when this state has been reached can important questions be raised, and only then may some aspect of science serve a particular inquiry. At this juncture some research by the educator may be in order, but that work should not be considered finished until the results have been proved by his or her own hands in the act of teaching.

In the introduction to this section of the book questions were raised: Is research impractical? Why is it that teachers prefer inspirational talks to reports on current research? The answer is that most of the research prescribed for education has been dreadfully impractical and inappropriate.

Teachers may seem a relatively humble lot, but the evidence is clear that they do eventually reject humbug.

Teachers will respond with enthusiasm to serious educational questions. When these are posed honestly and clearly, teachers will be ready to learn about the state of scientific knowledge. They will listen to reports of this kind eagerly, and they will understand them. Thereafter, the interpretations of this state of scientific knowledge will have to be carried out by teachers and for teachers. Presentations of this kind will not lack attention or attendance.

The only major writer in the field of reading to have presented research in psychology adequately for pedagogy is Huey. Serious teachers of reading still enjoy his text. He was a man of his age, and I have taken the liberty of quibbling with some of his views; in the main, however, his plan was a sound one and brilliantly executed. Despite our blunders, research in reading has moved forward in truly important ways. We begin to know the developmental path that children follow as they grow intellectually, as they master the conventions of text, and as they acquire control of the vocabulary of their written language. We are moving ever closer to understanding the basic controlling mechanism of language. We are able to describe the social conditions necessary for literacy and to track its history almost to the origins of language.

Let me end with a challenge. Let us find a team of young educators who respect the art of teaching and have the ability to learn and report clearly the state of our scientific knowledge of reading. Thereafter, let them discuss freely and fully the implications of this knowledge for reading instruction. This should require about five years of scholarly effort. Teachers would welcome such a work; so would publishers and parents. I hope the authors might decide to dedicate it to Edmund B. Huey.

The Researcher, Whole Language, and Reading

William D. Page

S ome researchers in reading are faced with the difficult task of accommodating a revivification of the whole language approach to reading and reading instruction. As if to increase the difficulties, the position is backed by sound evidence from qualitative studies with procedures that some researchers have made a career of criticizing. Small samples, introspection, and disregard for revered statistical procedures are characteristic of many of these qualitative studies. It is as though a great many professionals in reading had suddenly read Black's (*21*) warning over two decades ago that states, "The drastic simplifications demanded for success of the mathematical analysis entail a serious risk of confusing accuracy of the mathematics with strength of empirical verification in the original field" (p. 225). But the whole language movement is not simply a revolt against mathematical statistics, although some audiences always choose to reject what they don't understand because it would be troublesome for them to achieve competency with the ideas and procedures. No, Black's statement is not the result of a lack of understanding of mathematical statistics, and reading researchers are not in search of an easy end run.

What they seek is explanation. Descriptions of how reading works and how youngsters learn to read are required to permit teachers to plan, implement, and evaluate reading instruction. Such explanations can properly be called theory. Generating adequate theory requires research techniques that avoid reducing the scope of what is to be studied about reading and reading instruction to only those things that are amenable to quantification, the measurable and the observable. The search for explanations leads directly to qualitative studies, and, to some degree, away from quantitative studies. This is not a pejorative comment about quantification, mathematics, or statistics, but a recognition of the fact that different purposes often require different tools. If the purpose of a study is to explain a phenomenon that is not mathematics, then something in addition to, or other than, mathematics must be invoked. This simple truism also was recognized by Black when he wrote in relation to research, "Especially important is it to remember that the mathematical treatment furnishes no explanations" (p. 225).

What follows is a discussion of some of the predilections that must be addressed in approaching any statements about what researchers in reading should do. Accommodating the whole language view, the relationship between the reading theoretician and the reading researcher, and the use of wrong metaphors are also treated. Finally, some insights into sources of controversy are shared under the rubric of colliding lunatic fringes.

Predilections

The whole language view is intruding into reading. The concern is raised that the role of the reading researcher should be revised to accommodate this intrusion. The expression of this concern sets a common logical trap: that of tricking ourselves into thinking we can see into the future more clearly than is possible. What we say and write now can affect the thoughts of reading researchers of the future. Our statements become prescriptions telling reading researchers both how and what to think.

A prescription tells what should be. It differs from a description that tells what was, what is, or what will be if certain conditions prevail. The warrants required to support a descriptive claim are mustered from data. Mustering the required support for a prescription usually is more difficult because value systems as well as guesses about the future must be invoked.

In reading, we often begin work with a youngster who does not read, and literally get to watch his or her progress in developing reading ability. The longer range consequences of our work are not as easy to see. What are the academic consequences of our work? What are the economic consequences? What are the long range psychological consequences of our teaching? We may be unaware of the long range results of tinkering with the economic, academic, and psychological destinies of the youngsters for whom we are responsible.

Nobody predicts the future very well, not researchers and not teachers. However imperfect our feedback is on long range consequences, teachers are probably in a much better position than reading researchers to make judgments on the progress of our reading students. With respect to long range consequences, reading researchers probably can't predict the future any better then we can. Should they tell us what we should do in the future? Probably not. The question here is should we try to tell reading researchers what to do? Probably not!

We must be careful to couch our speculations about the future in the tentative voice of the scientist. The scientist's credibility depends on his or her ability to recognize and communicate the appropriate degree of fallibility that should be attached to any scientific conclusion, as well as offering the appropriate methodological support for the conclusion.

We know we can't look into the future. We know we can't influence what reading researchers do in the future. We know that science yields only tentative conclusions. So what do these ideas have to do with the concern at hand, the role of the reading researcher in relation to the concept of whole language as it relates to reading? The answer is that these ideas are critically important to any credible treatment of the role of the reading researcher in relation to any concept. We simply cannot predict or prescribe what reading researchers will or should do without pretending that we can look into the future in ways we know we cannot do.

For this reason, any description of the role of the reading researcher must be carefully qualified. Tomorrow, next year, a decade from now, someone will invent something that will dramatically change the way researchers will have to act in carrying out their work. What we present here makes sense only under the conditions that presently prevail. Any less tentative qualification is merely pretentious.

Accommodating the Whole Language View

In some sense, there is a science of science, a way of thinking about science and how it ought to be done. Sometimes it is called the methodology of science, metascience, or inquiry into inquiry (56). By whatever name we call it, it means that from time to time, when a new idea, technique, or tool emerges, we must reexamine the rules by which science is conducted to see if they still apply. If they do, then science proceeds on its way. If not, science must be adjusted to accommodate the new findings.

Adjustments are the rule, not the exception. Adjustments are in order not only when new ideas, techniques, or tools emerge, but also when old ideas that were rejected as invalid are reexamined in the light of new knowledge and subsequently revived. The concept of whole language is such an entity.

Certainly, whole language was considered many times in the past. Notably, Huey (137) recognized that manipulating words in isolation falls short of what people really do in language when he wrote, "The total idea of what is to be said thus exists in consciousness precedent to the utterance, and dominates the utterance throughout. This total idea is not a mere sum of associations, but it is an apperceptive unity" (p. 127). The concept of whole language as it applies to reading was in disfavor for a long time, but recently it underwent a revivication with respect to reading that demands adjustments. One area of adjustment is the role of the researcher. Perhaps the roles of the theoretician, the administrator, the teacher, the parent, and even the role of the student should also be reexamined.

What should researchers do that is different from what they are doing as a result of recognizing the revivication of whole-language concepts in reading theory? Of course, there are many answers to this question. We may scratch only the surface, but perhaps that is appropriate when attempting to reshape something as complex as researchers' roles. Some rethinking of the connection between reading research and theory and teaching appear to be required.

A reciprocal relationship of responsibility exists between researchers and teachers. The issues of this responsibility often center on communication. Why can't researchers write and speak so that teachers can understand what the researchers are trying to communicate? Why can't teachers prepare themselves to be competent consumers of research? These two questions are frequently asked in schools, research centers, universities, and editors' letters to authors.

The answers to these questions probably are not what either researchers or teachers are likely to expect. This chapter promises no conclusive settlement to the issues of communication between researchers and teachers, but some clarification is possible and even partial answers warrant the effort. Goodman (92) suggests roles other than the teacher, the researcher, and the theoretician. He describes the roles of the synthesizer, the innovator, the facilitator, and the disseminator. Perhaps we expect our researchers and teachers to perform competently in too many areas; thus, there may be a need to develop professionals to fulfill related but more specialized roles.

We get some insights from examining the preparation programs available for teachers and researchers. What are teachers taught to do? What are the skills researchers have at their command? We get some insights from examining the motivational structure in which teachers and researchers operate. For what are teachers rewarded? What is the reward system of researchers? What are the characteristics of the people who are close to teachers and researchers, and how do the support groups of each differ? Of course, full answers to these questions demand lifetimes of study, efforts far beyond the scope here; but perhaps it is time to begin asking the questions.

The Theoretician and the Researcher

The roles of the theoretician and the researcher can be understood a little better by examining what theory and research are thought to be. Some say theory is unproven statements. Many view it as sheer speculation, conclusions drawn in an armchair without encountering the phenomena to which the theory refers. Others see theory as a systematically related set of principles about the characteristics of phenomena. Still others describe theory as explanations of phenomena that are generated after encountering phenomena. For our purposes here, this last view is probably the most useful.

Like theory, research is viewed in many ways. Some see research as data handling. Chemists might be thought of as being nearly lost among their test tubes, glass loops, and beakers of steaming liquid. Others view research as the activity of archivists, aimless collectors of data for dusty volumes in old libraries. Still others imagine research to be quantification, representing the world in numbers and mathematical symbols. Here, researchers might be thought of as purposelessly counting everything countable, reducing their view of the world exclusively to what is countable, entering their counts into computers, and reveling in hundreds of feet of printout. Another view holds that researchers are systematic investigators of some area of knowledge. For our purposes, this last view is the most useful.

Several touchstones between theory and research become evident. Both theory and research use language. Language is used to propose projects to agencies for funding or doctoral theses to advisors for approval. The language of the proposals guides the work as it is carried out. Both researchers and theoreticians communicate their conclusions in language. Closely linked to language is another touchstone between theory and research, the fact that both theoreticians and researchers engage in epistemology. They share the overarching goal of trying to create new knowledge. Further, both treat only statements that are methodologically warranted as knowledge, although there is considerable disagreement both between and within groups of researchers and theoreticians about what constitutes adequate methodological warrant for believing a statement. Because both theory and research are guided by scientific theory, use theory to state their goals, and yield theory as their product, it is difficult to reconcile any major distinctions in their roles. The theorist encounters the phenomena of his or her concern and attempts to explain them. The researcher does the same thing. Goodman (92) uses physics as an example of a field where theoreticians and researchers are different people. In his view, the theorist proposes theory and the researcher confirms, disconfirms, or holds the theory in abeyance even after testing it. He suggests that "research produces unexpected findings that lead to modification, overthrow, or redevelopment of theory" (p. 141). This sounds as though the researchers produce theory as much as the theorists do and that the distinction between theorist and researcher may be less than clear even in physics.

In reading, Goodman maintains that "the reading process theorists are the researchers themselves—though not all researchers are involved in theory building" (p. 142). Since it is difficult to imagine a researcher who does not use statements to guide or to report his or her work and findings, it is difficult to conceive of a researcher not involved in theory building. Nevertheless, Goodman's point is important. His point might be stated another way by recognizing that researchers may turn their attentions to different theories even though they may be examining the same phenomena. Insights provided by Goodman suggest in the context of "a current renaissance of research on the reading process" (p. 143), that reading research has three purposes: "to study reading as a process,...to study reading development, that is, how people become readers, and...to study reading instruction" (p. 143). These three purposes stand as statements, instances of theory, that can guide theoreticians/researchers in reading.

Wrong Metaphors

Using a metaphor to gain insight into a phenomenon is so familiar to us that we sometimes forget that the two elements of the metaphor, the representer and the represented, are never perfectly isomorphic. We can't overemphasize this point. Postman (*180*) states, "In a fundamental sense, all arguments about how education ought to be conducted are arguments about the validity of competing metaphors." The trap of wrong metaphors is a concern as we approach the role of the reading researcher in relation to the concept of whole language. The architectural metaphor, comparing reading to a building, exhibits serious shortcomings that are the source of much of the controversy that persists between experimental and qualitative researchers with respect to whole language. The familiar armchair to work metaphor that casts the theoretician as a thinker in an armchair, the researcher as a discoverer, and the teacher as a doer on a continuum from theory to practice is quite peculiar when the real roles these individuals play are examined.

Much of the theory of reading and reading instruction relies heavily on the comparison of reading to some hypothetical building. Here, we refer to this comparison as the use of an architectural metaphor. Reading theory generated by the use of the architectural metaphor includes a host of references to parts of building. We read theory based on the architectural metaphor and find references to the foundations of reading, approaches to reading, levels of reading, entry and exit behaviors, and even windows on the reading process. Sometimes the architectural metaphor is useful for clarifying an idea. But sometimes it becomes a way of getting people to believe a misleading idea because the context of the metaphor is so familiar that the idea seems right.

Most buildings are constructed by transporting relatively small units of material to the building site one or a few at a time, locating the units in place according to a plan, and securing each unit to the others to form the whole building. Some of the units are solid such as bricks, boards, glass sheets, and steel beams. Some are flexible such as wire, asphalt shingles, and insulation blankets. Some are liquid such as unset concrete, glue, and paint. Usually a hole is dug, a foundation of concrete reinforced with steel is poured, and the superstructure of the building is attached to the foundation piece by piece. A building foundation that is too weak or poorly leveled may settle, collapse, tilt, or not be square with the world. As a result of this knowledge, society makes elaborate provisions for making sure foundations are made well through quality control of materials, building codes, and systems of building inspection at crucial points in the construction process.

Because people live in buildings, most are familiar to some degree with the results of the process of building construction. When the architectural construction metaphor for learning to read or teaching youngsters to read is used to try to explain the processes, our general familiarity with buildings takes over and we apply principles that work for buildings to reading, even where they don't work.

One principle that is applied regularly involves treating reading as a skill made up of subskills, just as a building is made up of smaller parts. Teaching the separate skills is assumed to be more easily accomplished if they are introduced one at a time, like the hods of bricks that are carried to the bricklayer. The bricklayer works from a plan to place the bricks in appropriate proximity to one another, securing each in its place with mortar. No such plan is available to the youngster because learning to read is not like constructing a building.

Reading exhibits no foundation in the sense that there are no identifiable building blocks of reading. If there is a foundation, it is the language the youngster brings to school from home, or the ability to understand the world, something he or she is equipped with from birth.

162   Page

The wide use of the architectural metaphor has contributed to the practice by both educators and reading researchers of trying to break reading down into manageable, measurable parts. Consider the fact that abstract skills are repeatedly shown to be more difficult to master than concrete skills. In reading or language related skill areas, we might substitute the ideas of immediately perceivable meaning for concrete. Immediately perceivable meaning is not possible unless meaning is available within the task the youngsters are asked to perform. An experience story is meaningful because the youngster can relate the written language to his or her experience and memory of writing about it. Phonics tasks involve relating meaningless sounds to graphic displays of meaningless letters and meaningless combinations of letters through an abstract system of over two hundred phonics rules—a difficult, highly abstract task indeed. Once language is fragmented, meaning usually disappears or becomes hopelessly distorted. Although the architectural metaphor for reading and learning to read may give us a sense of comfort and understanding in a domain of near chaos, it probably contributes to the chaos because the fit between architecture and reading is so poor.

The terms "armchair theorists," "clinical researcher," and "busy practitioner" frequently occur in the literature of reading instruction. It is as though a scientist can't theorize without an armchair, a researcher can't work without a clipboard and white laboratory smock, and the practitioner can't think because he or she is so busy. None of these postulated circumstances represents reality very often.

The term practical often becomes confused with practitioner, perhaps because both begin with the same first six letters and reading professionals have been inundated with phonemic-graphemic relationships for hundreds of years. It takes only one, short, illogical, leap to conclude that if practitioners are practical, those at the other end of the continuum, the armchair theorists, must be impractical. Few conclusions could be more wrong.

Consider what activities among the menu of possible things that people can do are most practical. Certainly, doing obvious physically observable tasks is considered practical by most people. However, doing the same tasks in a more efficient way through careful planning is considered more practical. Individuals who analyze the circumstances well enough to be able to eliminate a task altogether while achieving the same desired effect are considered very practical indeed. These individuals could be called theorists. They think through a circumstance and conclude that an approach which they have never witnessed can work. Who of these hypothetical beings is really most practical? Of course it is our thinkers.

What do thinkers use as their major tool? Language is the tool. What do they have to do with the language? They create descriptions of the circumstance of concern and guess about how it works, operates, or functions. These guesses are explanations, and explanations in language are instances of theory. Probably nothing that people do is more practical than creating theory, explanations of how things, including ourselves, work. The armchair to work, theorist to practitioner, metaphor does not represent reality.

Colliding Lunatic Fringes

In any complex human enterprise that involves large numbers of participants, it is usually possible to identify some people who might be classified by what they say, write, and do as nearly, if not actually, the "lunatic fringe." The group called reading researchers is not an exception. The "near" lunatic fringe is the source of outrageous statements, polemics, misguided attempts at self-aggrandizement, and controversy. It is also a source of new ideas, for when the cool, calm, comfortably collected scientists are backed into corners, they, like any other intelligent people, construct creative alternatives. Sometimes what appears to be part of the lunatic fringe is actually an instance of the rare problem creator making a first attempt to float out a new idea, to test reaction to it, and to learn what might be right or wrong about it from the criticisms of other scholars.

Most people participating in reading research today are likely to recognize at least two camps. One camp is identifiable with fragmented language, quantitative research, and behavioristic studies, a group of well trained researchers who espouse the methodologies that emanate from conventional experimental psychology. A second camp is identifiable with the whole language, qualitative research, and naturalistic studies, a group of well trained researchers who espouse the methodologies that emanate from anthropology, ethnography, and phenomenology. These quiet descriptions cloak the possibilities of emotion-ridden controversy that are sometimes characteristic of researchers' encounters with one another.

To remove the cloaks, all we need do is encounter statements that emerge from extreme factions of the two groups. One statement that was encountered at a recent national reading meeting is: "Only true experiments yield adequate knowledge." A second statement is: "No useful knowledge can be constructed from experimental studies in reading today." The former statement authoritatively came from the lips of a closet behaviorist wearing the cloak of a cognitive field psychologist at a meeting dominated by statisticians. The latter statement was pronounced with intonation suggesting conviction and authority by a whole language enthusiast. By simple logic, we can determine that because these statements are in direct conflict with one another, one or both of them must be wrong. Our contention here is that both statements are quite wrong. Further, they represent the near lunatic fringe conclusions that fire the controversies between the two camps, the fragmented language and whole language enthusiasts.

Perhaps some of the difficulties stem from the fact that these scholars let themselves become enthusiasts. They veered from their training which was supposed to have vaccinated them against subjectivity. The recipients of the messages expressed enthusiastic agreement in both instances. The issue is not really limited to concerns for objectivism over enthusiasm. The concept of methodology is useful for putting things into at least slightly better perspective. The true experiment is a tool designed to help construct new knowledge. No less a tool is the concept of naturalistic inquiry. Both have their origins firmly rooted in the practical considerations of epistemology, the name for the enterprise of making new knowledge.

Thinking of these two concepts as tools can help. Metaphorically, just because an individual has successfully driven nails with a hammer does not mean that he or she cannot appreciate and use a wrench to tighten a nut on a bolt, or a screwdriver to install a screw. We should choose the tools that fit the task. In reading research, the tool concept should fit the questions to be answered and the data to be encountered.

Conclusion

People often say that history repeats itself. This view of history is probably true in most instances, but not in all. Science exhibits a long history of self modification. We have no reason to believe that the tradition is going to change because of the intrusion of the revived concept of whole language as it applies to reading and reading instruction.

Science is a creative undertaking. It involves creating new knowledge. As such, each new probe into the unknown is an instance of creativity. The creative aspect of science applies to the methodology of science as well to the direct construction of knowledge in a conventional discipline. Demonstrating that a new way of analyzing data works results in new knowledge just as surely as new knowledge is created by demonstrating that a new reading test is valid, or that a new method of instruction helps youngsters learn to read more effectively.

The whole language approach to reading research is upon us. Because the whole language concept makes so much sense, and seems to be supplying us with new, useful insights through article after article, many who rejected it will change their minds. Of those who change their minds, some will adopt it and claim that it is what they believed all along. Those reading researchers who were using the whole language concept before its recent revivication may feel that the more recent converts are stealing their material, and not giving credit where it is due. This aspect of history does repeat itself with the emergence of each new idea. The concept of whole language as it applies to reading is probably here to stay for a long time.

Reading researchers will proceed as they see fit. Some will change their directions of emphases by the lure of various funding agencies. We hope the government will be in there competing for the attention of researchers, directing them to important problems. Some will find the logic of the whole language concept intriguing and pursue the conceptualization process for its own sake. We can expect very few to move toward a whole language position because anyone tells them to.

Researchers will continue to use language to write their proposals, to guide them in carrying out their research, and to report their findings. In short, researchers will continue to use theory in these ways. As such, researchers will continue to function as theorists.

Better metaphors will emerge. Some old ones will fall into disuse, while others will hang on despite poor fits. Some old metaphors will be retained because of their usefulness.

Controversy will remain with us as long as people with imagination remain interested in reading. We have no reason to anticipate a decline in imaginative people in reading. The lunatic fringes will probably remain at about the same proportions. People will disagree and argue, and we will know more about reading, how it works, and how people learn to do it than ever before.

A Postscript

I n spite of the many insightful ideas and concepts referred to in this volume regarding the reading process and how language is learned, most reading instruction in elementary schools continues to be based on the presupposition that children must consciously learn the "skills" of reading before they can read. Such instruction seems to be based on three assumptions which fail to recognize children's linguistic and cognitive abilities.

- Children do not have linguistic competence and therefore must be consciously taught about language – proceeding from part to whole – if their language performance is to improve.
- Children can deal with the abstractions inherent in the terms and conceptual ideas which accompany explicit language instruction.
- A knowledge of language terms, definitions and rules significantly improves language performance.

This point of view, however, does not seem to be supported by language learning research presented by the authors in this book. Instead, it would appear that children have powerful language learning abilities; reading "skills" are learned intuitively; such "skills" are a consequence of reading rather than prerequisites.

Holdaway (*130*) stressed the lack of attention given to reading as a language learning activity when he stated:

> The history of ideas in the acquisition of literacy is a history of competing methodologies focusing on teaching or instruction rather than on learning. In the past fifty years we have seen a revolution in knowledge about the nature of learning, yet in the vast literature on the teaching of reading, so voluminous that the dedicated student is threatened with verbal suffocation, there is seldom a mention of this knowledge. For instance, in the massive and influential study by Jeanne Chall, *Learning to Read: The Great Debate* (1967) or even in the 600 pages of The Bullock Report, *A Language for Life* (1975), only passing mention is made of how reading is actually learned. (p. 5)

Somehow, the notion that learning to read is simply a matter of "sounding out" or recognizing words in phrases, sentences and finally paragraphs and stories needs to be exchanged for a view that recognizes reading and learning to read as highly complex language processing activities. A child reading the following sentence with the many meanings, syntactical functions, and pronunciations for each word (*11*) must process the many variables in his/her "computer" to determine the one appropriate combination among the 96.6 quadrillion possible combinations that represent the author's intentions.

	Watch	the	dog	chase	the	cat	up	the	tree.
Meanings	23	10	23	17	10	24	40	10	15
Syntactical Functions	4	2	4	3	2	3	6	2	4
Pronunciations	1	3	1	1	3	1	1	3	1

How could this staggering psycholinguistic feat be accomplished without relying on the reader's linguistic genius, predictive powers, and use of the graphophonic, syntactic, and semantic cue systems?

Because of the discrepancies which exist between traditional teaching procedures and reading instruction more in keeping with language learning research, a phenomenon has emerged which might be termed the "180° Syndrome." That is, if traditional teaching procedures were reversed, they would then be more in line with language learning principles. For example, instead of learning words to read, read to learn words; instead of learning phonics to read, read to learn phonics; instead of having children read to their teacher to link visual patterns (print) they see with their knowledge of the world and phonological rules, the teacher should read to the children; and instead of comprehension questions coming from teachers and materials, children should generate their own questions which reflect their cognitive development, experiential background and interests.

During a recent NIE Hearing on Language and Literacy, Anderson (5) estimated that 96 percent of the reading instruction in the United States (grades 1-8) was based on commercial basal programs which do not reflect sound instructional design for reading and learning. Only 1 percent of the instruction incorporated teacher devised materials and trade books. How can this circumstance be changed? What changes need to be initiated so that teachers will be respected as competent professionals who are capable of involving their students appropriately in the reading process? Must we be content with the ludicrous lag between practice and research?

In Chapter 11, Stratton describes how the Ontario Ministry of Education developed guidelines and policies based upon the cognitive development of children and language as process. McKenzie (Chapter 12) also referred to the top down format used in London for bringing about curricular change. Having the "weight of the law" in support of theoretically sound teaching might well be what it will take to motivate teachers to begin thinking about why they teach as they do, and to encourage administrators and supervisors to develop long term indepth inservice offerings which go beyond the "one shot" superficial and fragmented presentation which has typified most inservice efforts to date. Administrators' efforts to remove the we-they syndrome also need to be rewarded if the cooperative effort described in this book is to be realized.

If ideas such as those discussed in this book are to influence teacher behavior and educational policy, they need to be brought to the attention of legislators and members of boards of education. For too long a few zealous teachers have been trying in vain to initiate curricular change in a system which reveres teacher proof materials and fails to recognize teachers as decision makers. Who will dare to lobby for more enlightened educational policies and practices? Perhaps if such policies were adopted, literacy instruction would then become more of an ongoing cooperative effort appropriately reflecting the roles, specialized knowledge, skills, and abilities of all those involved.

References

1. Adelman, C. (Ed.). *Uttering, Muttering.* London: Grant McIntyre, 1981.
2. Allington, R.L. "Poor Readers Don't Get to Read Much in Reading Groups," *Language Arts,* 57 (1980a), 872-876.
3. Allington, R.L. "Teacher Interruption Behaviors During Primary Grade Oral Reading," *Journal of Educational Psychology,* 72 (1980b), 371-377.
4. Almy, M.C. "Young Children's Thinking and the Teaching of Reading," in Joe L. Frost (Ed.), *Issues and Innovations: The Teaching of Reading.* Glenview, IL: Scott, Foresman, 1967.
5. Anderson, R.C. *Report in United States Department of Education Staff Summary, Hearing on Language and Literacy.* Houston, TX: 1982.
6. Applebee, A.N. "Children and Stories: Learning the Rules of the Game," *Language Arts,* 56 (1979), 641-646.
7. Applebee, A.N. *The Child's Concept of Story.* Chicago: University of Chicago Press, 1978.
8. Athey, I. "Synthesis of Papers on Language Development and Reading," *Reading Research Quarterly,* 7 (Fall 1971).
9. Barnes, D. *From Communication to Curriculum,* Harmondsworth, England: Penguin, 1976, 90-91.
10. Barnes, W.G. "The Developmental Acquisition of Silent Letters and Orthographic Images in English Spelling," unpublished doctoral dissertation, University of Virginia at Charlottesville, 1982.
11. Barnhart, C.L. (Ed.). *The World Book Dictionary.* Chicago: Field Enterprises, 1969.
12. Barrett, F.L. *A Teacher's Guide to Shared Reading.* Toronto: Scholastic, 1982.
13. Barron, R. "Development of Visual Word Recognition: A Review," *Reading Research in Theory and Practice,* Vol. 3. New York: Academic Press, 1981.
14. Barthes, R. *Le Plaisir du Texte.* Paris: Senil, 1975.
15. Barthes, R. *The Pleasure of the Text.* London: Cape, 1976.
16. Bear, D. "Patterns of Oral Reading Across Stages of Word Knowledge," unpublished doctoral dissertation, University of Virginia at Charlottesville, 1982.
17. Benton, M. "Children's Responses to Stories," *Children's Literature in Education,* 10 (1979), 68-85.
18. Bettelheim, B., and K. Zelan. *On Learning to Read.* New York: Alfred Knopf, 1981.
19. Bissex, G.L. GNYS *at* WRK: *A Child Learns to Write and Read.* Cambridge, MA: Harvard University Press, 1980.
20. Bissex, G.L. "Learning to Write and Read: A Case Study," unpublished doctoral dissertation, Harvard University, 1979.
21. Black, M. *Models and Metaphors.* Ithaca, New York: Cornell University Press, 1962.
22. Bloomfield, L. *Language.* New York: H. Holt, 1933.
23. Board, P. "Toward a Theory of Instructional Influence: Aspects of the Instructional Environment and Their Influence on Children's Acquisition of Reading," unpublished doctoral dissertation, University of Toronto, 1982.

24. Booth, W. *The Knowledge Most Worth Having*. Chicago: University of Chicago Press, 1967.
25. Borko, H., R.J. Shavelson, and P. Stern. "Teachers' Decisions in the Planning of Reading Instruction," *Reading Research Quarterly*, 16 (1981), 449-466.
26. Bradley, H. *On the Relations Between Spoken and Written Language with Special Reference to English*. Proceedings of the British Academy, Volume 6. London: Oxford University Press, 1918.
27. Britton, J. *Language and Learning*. London: Allen Lane, Penguin Press, 1970.
28. Brown, E. "A Theory of Reading," *Journal of Communication Disorders*, 14 (1981), 443-466.
29. Browne, M.P.J. "An Exploratory Study of Teacher-Pupil Verbal Interaction in Primary Reading Groups," unpublished doctoral dissertation, University of Alberta, 1971.
30. Bullock Report. *A Language for Life*. London: HMSO, 1975.
31. Burnett, F.H. "Literature and the Doll," in *Surly Tim and Other Stories*. New York: C. Scribner Sons, 1914.
32. Burton, F., and S. DeLapp. "Literary Links to Writing," paper presented at the Second Annual Children's Literature Conference, Columbus, Ohio, 1984.
33. Bussis, Anne M., Edward A. Chittenden, and Marianne Amarel. *Beyond Surface Curriculum: An Interview Study of Teachers' Understandings*. Boulder, CO: Westview Press, 1976.
34. Cahir, S.R., and C. Kovacs. *Exploring Functional Language*. Washington, D.C.: Center for Applied Linguistics, 1981.
35. Carrier, J. "Masking the Social in Educational Knowledge: The Case of Learning Disability Theory," *American Journal of Sociology*, December 1984.
36. Cazden, C.B. "Peekaboo as an Instructional Model: Discourse Development at Home and at School," *Papers and Reports on Child Language Development*, No. 17. Palo Alto, CA: Stanford University, 1979. (ED 191 274)
37. Cazden, Courtney B. "Suggestions for Studies of Early Language Acquisition," *Language in Early Childhood Education*. Washington, DC: National Association for the Education of Young Children, 1972.
38. Chall, Jeanne. *Learning to Read: The Great Debate*. New York: McGraw-Hill, 1967.
39. Chomsky, Carol. "How Sister Got into the Grog," *Early Years*, November 1975.
40. Chomsky, Carol. "States in Language Development and Reading Exposure," *Harvard Educational Review*, 42 (1972), 1-33.
41. Chomsky, Noam. "A Review of B. F. Skinner's Verbal Behavior," *Language*, 35 (1959), 26-58, reprint.
42. Chomsky, Noam. *Syntactic Structures*. The Hague: Mouton, 1957.
43. Clark, Margaret M. *Young Fluent Readers*. London: Heinemann, 1976.
44. Clay, Marie M. *A Diagnostic Survey*. London: Heinemann, 1972.
45. Clay, Marie M. *Reading: The Patterning of Complex Behaviour*. Auckland, NZ: Heinemann, 1973.
46. Clay, Marie M. *What Did I Write?* Auckland, NZ: Heinemann, 1976.
47. CLPE Publications. J. Jurica. *Language Matters* and *Tried and Tested*. Both published three times a year by the Centre for Language in Primary Education, Sutherland Street, London, SW1V 4LH.
48. Cochran-Smith, M. Doctoral dissertation, University of Pennsylvania, 1976.
49. Cohn, M. "Observations of Learning to Read," *Language Arts*, 58 (1981), 549-556.
50. Conrad, Joseph. *Typhoon and Youth*. Bath: Lythway Press, 1976.
51. Cook-Gumperz, J., and J. Gumperz. "From Oral to Written Culture: The Transition to Literacy," in Marcia Farr Whiteman (Ed.), *Writing: The Nature, Development, and Teaching of Written Communication*. Hillsdale, NJ: Erlbaum, 1981.
52. Craig, G. "Reading: Who Does What to Whom," in C. Josipovici (Ed.), *The Modern English Novel*. London: Open Books, 1978.

References   171

53. DeFord, D.E. "Young Children and Their Writing," *Theory into Practice,* 19 (Summer 1980), 157-169.
54. DeLapp, S.R. "Dilemmas of Teaching: A Self-Reflective Analysis of Teaching in a Third-Fourth Grade Informal Classroom," unpublished doctoral dissertation, Ohio State University, 1980.
55. Dewey, J. *Democracy and Education.* New York: Macmillan, 1916.
56. Dewey, J. *Logic: The Theory of Inquiry.* New York: Holt, Rinehart and Winston, 1938.
57. Dillon, D., and D. Searle. "The Role of Language in One First Grade Classroom," *Research in the Teaching of English,* 15 (1981), 311-328.
58. Doake, D.B. "Book Experience and Emergent Reading Behavior in Preschool Children," unpublished doctoral dissertation, University of Alberta, 1981.
59. Dombey, H. "Learning the Language of the Book," *Bedford Way Papers.* London: Institute of Education, 1983.
60. Donaldson, M. *Children's Minds.* London: Fontana/Croom Helm, 1978.
61. Downing, J. *Reading and Reasoning.* New York: Springer-Verlag, 1979.
62. Downing, J. "Words, Words, Words," *Theory into Practice,* 16 (1977), 325-333.
63. Downing, J., L. Ollila, and P. Oliver. "Concepts of Language in Children from Differing Socioeconomic Backgrounds," *Journal of Educational Research,* 70 (1977), 277-281.
64. Duffy, G.G., and L.R. Roehler. "Commentary: The Illusion of Instruction," *Reading Research Quarterly,* 17 (1982), 438-445.
65. Dunn, R., and K. Dunn. *Teaching Students through Their Individual Learning Styles: A Practical Approach.* Reston, VA: Reston Publishing, 1978.
66. Durkin, D. *Children Who Read Early.* New York: Teachers College Press, 1966.
67. Durkin, D. "Reading Comprehension Instruction in Five Basal Series," *Reading Research Quarterly,* 16 (1981) 515-544.
68. Durkin, D. "What Classroom Observations Reveal about Reading Comprehension Instruction," *Reading Research Quarterly,* 14 (1978-1979), 481-533.
69. Dworkin, M. *Dewey on Education.* New York: Teachers College Press, 1966.
70. Edwards, A.D. "Perspectives: Language Difference and Educational Failure," *Language Arts,* May 1982, 513-519.
71. Ehri, L. "The Development of Orthographic Images," in U. Frith (Ed.), *Cognitive Processes in Spelling.* London: Academic Press, 1980.
72. Ehri, L. "The Role of Orthographic Images in Learning Printed Words," in J. Kavanagh and R. Venezky (Eds.), *Orthography, Reading, and Dyslexia.* Baltimore: University Park Press, 1980.
73. Elkind, D. *A Sympathetic Understanding of the Child: Birth to Sixteen.* Boston, MA: Allyn and Bacon, 1974.
74. Elkind, D. *Children and Adolescents: Interpretive Essays on Jean Piaget.* New York: Oxford Press, 1974.
75. Emans, R. "Congressional Oversight Hearings," June 18, 1981. Also in *Epistle,* Fall/Winter, 1981, 2-16; and *Journal of Teacher Education,* July/August 1982, 16-21.
76. Emans, R. "Emphasizing Reading Skills in an English Course for Underachievers," *Journal of Reading,* February 1969, 373-376, 414-415.
77. Emans, R. "What Do Children in the Inner City Like to Read?" *Elementary School Journal,* December 1968, 119-122.
78. Entwistle, D. "Implications of Language: Socialization for Reading Models and for Learning to Read," *Reading Research Quarterly,* 7 (Fall 1971).
79. Epstein, H.T. "Growth Spurts During Brain Development: Implications for Educational Policy and Practice," *Education and the Brain.* Seventy-Seventh Yearbook of the National Society for the Study of Education. Chicago: University of Chicago Press, 1978.

80. Erickson, F., and J. Shultz. "When Is a Context? Some Issues and Methods in the Analysis of Social Competence," in J. Green and C. Wallet (Eds.), *Ethnography and Language in Educational Settings*. Norwood, NJ: Ablex, 1981.
81. Fernald, G.M. *Remedial Techniques in Basic School Subjects*. New York: McGraw-Hill, 1943.
82. Fisher, D.L. *Functional Literacy and the Schools*. Washington, DC: National Institute of Education, 1978.
83. Florio, S., and C.M. Clark. "The Functions of Writing in an Elementary Classroom," *Research in the Teaching of English*, 16 (May 1982), 115-130.
84. Fox, C. "Talking Like a Book," *Bedford Way Papers*. London: Institute of Education, 1983.
85. French, M.A. "Observations on the Chinese Script and the Classification of Writing Systems," in W. Haas (Ed.), *Writing without Letters*. United Kingdom: Manchester University Press, 1976.
86. Gardner, K. "Early Reading Skills," in K. Gardner (Ed.), *Reading Skills: Theory and Practice*. London: Ward Lock, 1970.
87. Gelb, I.T. *A Study of Writing*. Chicago: University of Chicago Press, 1952.
88. Geschwind, N. *Selected Papers on Language and the Brain*. Boston: D. Reidel Publishing, 1974.
89. Gillingham, A., and B. Stillman. "Remedial Teaching for Children with Specific Disability," in *Reading, Spelling, and Penmanship*. Cambridge: Educators' Publishing Services, 1968.
90. Goffman, E. *Forms of Talk*. Philadelphia: University of Pennsylvania, 1980.
91. Goodman, K.S. "Acquiring Literacy Is Natural: Who Skilled Cock Robin?" *Theory into Practice*, 16 (1977), 309-314.
92. Goodman, K. "Bridging the Gaps in Reading: Respect in Communication," in Jerome Harste and Robert Carey (Eds.), *New Perspectives on Comprehension*. Monograph in Language and Reading Studies, October 1979. Bloomington: Indiana University Press. 1979.
93. Goodman, K.S. "Effective Teachers of Reading Know Language and Children," *Elementary English*, September 1974, 823.
94. Goodman, K.S. "Language and Literacy: The Selected Writings of Kenneth S. Goodman," Volume 1, *Process, Theory and Research*, edited and introduced by Frederick V. Gollasch. Boston: RKP, 1982.
95. Goodman, K.S. "Reading: A Psycholinguistic Guessing Game," *Journal of Reading Specialist*, 4 (1967), 126-135.
96. Goodman, K.S., with C. Buck. "Dialect Barriers to Reading Comprehension Revisited," *Reading Teacher*, 27 (1973), 8-12.
97. Goodman, K., and Y. Goodman. *A Whole Language Comprehension Centered Reading Program*. Occasional Paper, Program in Language and Literacy, University of Arizona, 1981.
98. Goodman, Y., and B. Altwerger. *Print Awareness in Preschool Children: A Study of the Development of Literacy in Preschool Children*. Occasional Paper, Program in Language and Literacy, University of Arizona, 1981.
99. Goodman, Y., and C. Burke. *Reading Strategies: Focus on Comprehension*. New York: Holt, Rinehart and Winston, 1980.
100. Goody, J., and I. Watt. *Literacy in Traditional Societies*. London: Cambridge University Press, 1978.
101. Graves, D.H. *Balance the Basics: Let Them Write*. New York: Ford Foundation, 1978.
102. Graves, D.H. "An Examination of the Writing Processes of Seven Year Old Children," *Research in the Teaching of English*, 9 (Winter 1975), 227-241.
103. Graves, D.H. *Writing: Teachers and Children at Work*. Exeter, NH: Heinemann, 1983.

104. Gray, W., and B. Rogers. *Maturity in Reading, Its Nature and Appraisal.* Chicago: University of Chicago Press, 1964.
105. Green, H.A., and W.T. Petty. *Developing Language Skills in the Elementary Schools,* Fifth Edition. Boston: Allyn and Bacon, 1975.
106. Green, J.L., and D. Smith. "Teaching and Learning: A Linguistic Perspective," *Elementary School Journal,* 83 (1983), 353-391.
107. Gumperz, J. "Sociocultural Knowing in Conversational Inference," in M. Saville-Troike (Ed.), *Twenty-Eighth Annual Round Table Monograph Series on Language and Linguistics.* Washington, DC: Georgetown University Press, 1977.
108. Guszak, F.J. "Teacher Questioning and Reading," *Reading Teacher,* 1967, 227-234.
109. Haberman, M. *The Legacy of Teacher Education, 1980-2000.* Washington, DC: American Association of Colleges for Teacher Education, 1981.
110. Halliday, M.A.K. *Explorations in the Functions of Language.* London: Edward Arnold, 1973.
111. Halliday, M.A.K. "Learning How to Mean," in E.H. Lenneberg and E. Lenneberg (Eds.), *Language Development,* Volume 1. New York: Academic Press, 1975.
112. Halliday, M.A.K. "Relevant Models of Language," *Educational Review,* 22 (November 1969).
113. Handy, L., and D. Holdaway. *Teacher's Manual: Read-It-Again Series.* Sydney: Ashton Scholastic, 1980.
114. Harste, J.C., and C. Burke. "A New Hypothesis for Reading Teacher Research: Both Teaching and Learning of Reading Are Theoretically Based," in P. David Pearson (Ed.), *Reading: Theory, Research, and Practice.* Clemson, SC: National Reading Conference, 1977, 32-40.
115. Harste, J.C., C.L. Burke, and V.A. Woodward. "Children's Language and World: Initial Encounters with Print," in J. Langer and M.T. Smith-Burke (Eds.), *Reader Meets Author/Bridging the Gap.* Newark, DE: International Reading Association, 1982.
116. Harste, J., and L. Rhodes. "Viewpoints," *Language Arts,* 1982.
117. Harste, J., V. Woodward, and C. Burke. "Examining Our Assumptions: A Transactional View of Literacy and Learning," *Research in the Teaching of English,* 18 (February 1984), 84-108.
118. Harvey, W.L., and M. Mix. *Daily Lesson Plans,* The Horace Mann Readers. New York: Longman, Green, 1912.
119. Heath, S.B. *Ways with Words: Language, Life, and Work in Communities and Classrooms.* New York: Cambridge University Press, 1983.
120. Heath, S.B. "What No Bedtime Story Means: Narrative Skills at Home and School," *Language in Society,* 11 (1982), 49-70.
121. Hebb, D. *Organization of Behavior: A Neuropsychological Theory.* New York: Wiley, 1949.
122. Henderson, E.H. "A Study of Individually Formulated Purposes for Reading," *Journal of Educational Research,* 58 (1965), 438-441.
123. Henderson, E.H. *Teaching Children to Spell English.* Boston: Houghton Mifflin, 1984.
124. Henderson, E.H., and J. Beers. *Developmental and Cognitive Aspects of Learning to Spell: A Reflection of Word Knowledge.* Newark, DE: International Reading Association, 1981.
125. Hepler, S.I. "Patterns of Response to Literature: A One Year Study of a Fifth and Sixth Grade Classroom," unpublished doctoral dissertation, Ohio State University, 1980.
126. Hickman, J. "A New Perspective on Response to Literature: Research in an Elementary School Setting," *Research in the Teaching of English,* 15 (December 1981), 343-354.
127. Hickman, J.G. "Response to Literature in a School Environment, Grades K-5," unpublished doctoral dissertation, Ohio State University, 1979.
128. Hiebert, E.H. "Developmental Patterns and Interrelationships of Preschool Children's Print Awareness," *Reading Research Quarterly,* 16 (1981), 236-260.
129. Hodges, R.E. "Research Update: On the Development of Spelling Ability," *Language Arts,* March 1982, 284-290.

130. Holdaway, D. *The Foundations of Literacy.* Sydney: Ashton Scholastic, 1979.
131. Holdaway, D. *Independence in Reading,* Second Edition. Sydney: Ashton Scholastic, 1980.
132. Hoole, C. *A New Discovery of the Old Art of Teaching School.* Menston, England: Scolan Press, 1969.
133. Hoskisson, K. "Should Parents Teach Their Children to Read?" *Elementary English,* 51 (1974), 295.
134. Hough, R., and J. Nurss. "Effects of an Integrated Language Arts Program on the Oral Language of Kindergarten through Third Grade Children: A Pilot Study." Research report, Georgia State University, Atlanta, September 1982.
135. Howsam, R.B., D.C. Corrigan, G.W. Denemark, and R.J. Nash. *Educating a Profession.* Washington, DC: American Association for Colleges of Teacher Education, 1976.
136. Huck, C.S. *Children's Literature in the Elementary School,* Fourth Edition. New York: Holt, Rinehart and Winston, 1982.
137. Huey, E. *The Psychology and Pedagogy of Reading.* Cambridge, MA: MIT Press, 1968. First published by Macmillan, 1908.
138. Hymes, D. *Foundations in Sociolinguistics.* Philadelphia: University of Pennsylvania Press, 1974.
139. James, W. *Talks to Teachers on Psychology, and to Students on Some of Life's Ideals.* New York: Norton, 1958.
140. Kerlinger, F.N. *Foundations of Behavioral Research.* New York: Holt, Rinehart and Winston, 1973.
141. Kermode, F. *The Genesis of Secrecy.* Cambridge, MA: Harvard University Press, 1980.
142. King, M.L. "Evaluating Reading," *Theory into Practice,* 16 (1977), 407-418.
143. King, M.L., and V.M. Rentel. *How Children Learn to Write: A Longitudinal Study.* Washington, DC: National Institute of Education, 1981.
144. Kodaly System. Chosky, Lois. *The Kodaly Context: Creating an Environment for Musical Learning.* Englewood Cliffs, NJ: Prentice-Hall, 1981.
145. Langer, S.K. *Mind: An Essay on Human Feeling.* Baltimore: Johns Hopkins Press, 1973.
146. Langer, S.K. *Philosophy and a New Key,* Third Edition. Cambridge, MA: Harvard University Press, 1971.
147. Larrick, N. *Encourage Your Child to Read: A Parent's Guide to Children's Reading.* New York: Dell, 1980.
148. Lieberman, P. *Speech Physiology and Acoustic Phonetics.* New York: Macmillan, 1977.
149. Lieberman, P. *An Introduction to the Origins of Language.* New York: Macmillan, 1975.
150. Lenneberg, E. *Biological Foundations of Language.* New York: John Wiley and Sons, 1967.
151. Lozanov, G. *Suggestology.* New York: Gordon and Breach, 1976.
152. Martin, B., Jr., and P. Brogan. *Teacher's Guide, Instant Readers.* New York: Holt, Rinehart and Winston, 1972.
153. Massaro, D. *Understanding Language: An Information Processing Analysis of Speech Perception, Reading, and Psycholinguistics.* New York: Academic Press, 1975.
154. Mayne, W. *The Blue Book of Hob Stories.* New York: Philomel Books, 1984.
155. McConkle, G. "What the Study of Eye Movement Reveals about Reading," in L. Resnick and P. Weaver (Eds.), *Theory and Practice of Early Reading.* Hillsdale, NJ: Erlbaum, 1979.
156. McCracken, R.A., and M.J. McCracken. *Reading Is Only the Tiger's Tail.* San Rafael, CA: Lewing Press, 1972.
157. McKay, D.C. "The Structure of Words and Syllables: Evidence from Errors in Speech," *Cognitive Psychology,* 3 (1972), 210-227.

158. McLean, J.E., and L.K. Snyder-McLean. *A Transactional Approach to Early Language Training.* Columbus, OH: Charles E. Merrill, 1978.
159. McNeill, D. *The Acquisition of Language: The Study of Developmental Psycholinguistics.* New York: Harper and Row, 1970.
160. Mearns, H. *Creative Power.* New York: Dover, 1958.
161. Meek, M. *Achieving Literacy: Longitudinal Studies of Adolescents Learning to Read.* London: Routledge and Kegan, 1983.
162. Meek, M. *Learning to Read.* London: The Bodley Head, 1982.
163. Meek, M., A. Warlow, and G. Barton. *The Cool Web: The Pattern of Children's Reading.* London: The Bodley Head, 1977.
164. Menyuk, Paula. *The Acquisition and Development of Language.* Englewood Cliffs, NJ: Prentice-Hall, 1971.
165. Miller, G.A. *Spontaneous Apprentices.* New York: Seabury Press, 1977.
166. Moffett, J. *Teaching the Universe of Discourse.* Boston: Houghton Mifflin, 1968.
167. Murrow, C., and L. Murrow. *Children Come First.* New York: Harper and Row, 1971.
168. Ninio, A., and J. Bruner. "The Achievement and Antecedents of Labelling," *Child Language,* 5 (1976), 1-15.
169. Ornstein, S., and L. Schroeder. *Superlearning.* New York: Dell, 1979.
170. Pennfield, W., and L. Roberts. *Speech and Brain Mechanisms.* Princeton, NJ: Princeton University Press, 1959.
171. Petty, W.T., and J.M. Jensen. *Developing Children's Language.* Boston: Allyn and Bacon, 1980.
172. Phelps, W.L. *Autobiography with Letters.* New York: Oxford University Press, 1939.
173. Piaget, J. *The Child's Conception of the World.* London: Routledge and Kegan Paul, 1929.
174. Piaget, J. "To Understand Is to Invent," *Manas,* January 30, 1974.
175. Pinnell, G.S. "Language in Primary Classrooms," *Theory into Practice,* December 1975.
176. Pitman, J. *Alphabets and Reading: The Initial Teaching Alphabet.* London: Pitman and Sons, 1969.
177. Platt, Nancy G. "The Context for Writing: A Descriptive Study of One Family Grouped Informal First and Second Grade Classroom," unpublished doctoral dissertation, Ohio State University, 1982.
178. Plessas, G., and C. Oakes. "Prereading Experiences of Selected Early Readers," *Reading Teacher,* 17 (1964), 241-245.
179. Plowden Report. *Children and Their Primary Schools.* London: HMSO Publishers, 1967.
180. Postman, N. *Teaching as a Conserving Activity.* New York: Delta, 1979.
181. Prebram, K. *Language of the Brain.* Englewood Cliffs, NJ: Prentice-Hall, 1971.
182. *Primary Education in England.* A Survey by Her Majesty's Inspectors of Schools. London: HMSO Publishers, 1978.
183. Read, C. "Children's Judgments of Phonetic Similarities in Relation to English Spelling," *Language Learning,* 23 (June 1973), 17-38.
184. Read, C. *Children's Categorizations of Speech Sounds in English.* Research Report No. 17. Urbana, IL: National Council of Teachers of English, 1975.
185. Reed, M.D. "Children's and Teachers' Recall and Reactions to Read Aloud Books," unpublished doctoral dissertation, Ohio State University, 1979.
186. Reed, M.D. "A Community of Teachers," *English Education,* 9 (Winter 1978), 95-101.
187. Reed, M.D. "Language and Learning through Authentic Experiences: A Thematic Approach to Integrated Meaning," *Insights into Open Education,* 10 (October 1977), 6-12.
188. Reed, M.D. "Reading in the Open Classroom," *Theory into Practice,* 16 (December 1977), 392-400.

189. Reid, J.F. "Learning to Think about Reading," *Educational Research,* 9 (1966), 56-62; A. Melnik and J. Merritt. *Reading Today and Tomorrow.* University of London Press, in association with Open University Press, 1972.
190. Rhodes, L.K. "I Can Read! Predictable Books as Resources for Reading and Writing Instruction," *Reading Teacher,* 34 (1981), 511-518.
191. Richards, I.A. *How to Read a Page.* London: Routledge and Kegan, 1929.
192. Robinson, H. Alan. "Reading Instruction and Research: In Historical Perspective," in H. Alan Robinson (Ed.), *Reading and Writing Instruction in the United States: Historical Trends.* Newark, DE: International Reading Association. Urbana, IL: Eric Clearinghouse on Reading and Communications Skills, 1977.
193. Rogers, C.R. *Freedom to Learn.* Columbus, OH: Charles E. Merrill, 1969.
194. Rosen, H. "Written Language and the Sense of Audience," *Educational Research,* 15 (June 1973).
195. Rosenshine, B.V. "Content, Time, and Direct Instruction," in P.L. Peterson and H.J. Walberg (Eds.), *Research on Teaching: Concepts, Findings, and Implications.* Berkeley, CA: McCutchan, 1979.
196. Santin, S. "The Language of Teachers of Young Mentally Retarded Children in the Classroom," unpublished doctoral dissertation, University of Toronto, 1982.
197. Sartre, J.P. *Les Mots.* Paris: Gallimand, 1964.
198. Schickedanz, J. "Please Read that Story Again," *Young Children,* December 1978.
199. Schlagal, R.C. "A Qualitative Inventory of Word Knowledge: A Developmental Study of Spelling, Grades One through Six," unpublished doctoral dissertation, University of Virginia, 1982.
200. Schuster, D.H., R. Benitex-Borden, and C.A. Gritton. *Suggestive, Accelerative Learning and Teaching: A Manual of Classroom Procedures Based on the Lozanov Method.* Ames, IA: Society for Suggestive-Accelerative Learning and Teaching, 1976.
201. Schwab, J.J. "The Practical: A Language for Curriculum," *School Review,* November 1969, 1-23.
202. Scribner, S., and M. Cole. *The Psychology of Literacy.* Cambridge, MA: Harvard University Press, 1981.
203. Silberman, C.E. *Crisis in the Classroom.* New York: Random House, 1970.
204. Sinclair, J., and R.M. Coulthard. *Towards an Analysis of Discourse.* London: Oxford University Press, 1975.
205. Smith, B. *A Design for a School of Pedagogy.* Washington, DC: Government Printing Office, 1980.
206. Smith, F. "Demonstrations, Engagements, and Sensitivity: The Choice between People and Programs," *Language Arts,* 58 (1981), 634-642.
207. Smith, F. *Comprehension and Learning: A Conceptual Framework for Teachers.* New York: Holt, Rinehart and Winston, 1975.
208. Smith, F. *Essays into Literacy.* Exeter, NH: Heinemann, 1983.
209. Smith, F. *Reading without Nonsense.* New York: Teachers College Press, 1979.
210. Smith, F. *Understanding Reading,* Third Edition. New York: Holt, Rinehart and Winston, 1982.
211. Smith, F. *Writing and the Writer.* New York: Holt, Rinehart and Winston, 1982.
212. Snow, C.E., and B.A. Goldfield. "Turn the Page, Please: Situation-Specific Language Acquisition," unpublished manuscript, Harvard University.
213. Soderbergh, R. "Learning to Read Between Two and Five: Some Observations on Normal Hearing and Deaf Children," a paper presented at the Georgetown University Round Table on Language and Linguistics, 1976.
214. Spoehr, K., and E. Smith. "The Role of Syllables in Perceptual Processing," *Cognitive Psychology,* 5 (1975), 71-89.
215. Stauffer, R.G. *The Language Experience Approach to the Teaching of Reading.* New York: Harper and Row, 1980.

216. Stauffer, R.G., J.C. Abrams, and T.T. Pikulski. *Diagnosis, Correction and Prevention of Reading Disabilities.* New York: Harper and Row, 1978.
217. Stauffer, R.G., and W.D. Hammond. "The Effectiveness of Language Arts and Basic Reader Approaches to First Grade Reading Instruction—Extended into Third Grade," *Reading Research Quarterly,* 4 (Summer 1969), 468-499.
218. Steinberg, D.D., and W.T. Steinberg. "Reading before Speaking," *Visible Language,* 9 (1975), 197-224.
219. Stross, B. "Language Acquisition and Teaching," *Language Arts,* 55 (1978), 749-755.
220. Suzuki, S. *Nurtured by Love: A New Approach to Education.* New York: Exposition Press, 1969.
221. Taylor, D. *Family Literacy.* Exeter, NH: Heinemann, 1983.
222. Taylor, N.E., I.H. Blum, D.M. Logsdon, and G.D. Moeller. "The Development of Written Language Awareness: Environmental Aspects and Program Characteristics," paper presented at American Educational Research Association, New York, 1982.
223. Teale, T.H. "Literacy Activities in the Homes of Low Income Preschool Children," paper presented at conference on home influences and home achievement, Madison, Wisconsin, October 1981.
224. Teale, T.H., E. Estrada, and A.B. Anderson. "How Preschoolers Interact with Written Communication," in M.L. Kamil and A. Moe (Eds.), *Directions in Reading: Research and Instruction.* Washington, DC: National Reading Conference, 1981.
225. Teale, W. "Parents Reading to Their Children: What We Know and Need to Know," *Language Arts,* 58 (1981), 902-912.
226. Temple, C.A., R.G. Nathan, and N.A. Burris. *The Beginnings of Writing.* Boston: Allyn and Bacon, 1982.
227. *Theory into Practice.* "Learning to Write: An Expression of Language," 19 (Summer 1980). "Reading and Language," 16 (December 1977); "Children's Literature," 21 (Autumn 1982), Ohio State University.
228. Tolkien, J.R.R. *Tree and Leaf.* London: Allen and Unwin, 1964.
229. Tolstoy, A. *The Great Big Enormous Turnip.* Glenview, IL: Scott, Foresman, 1971.
230. Torrey, J. "Learning to Read without a Teacher," in F. Smith (Ed.), *Psycholinguistics and Reading.* New York: Holt, Rinehart and Winston, 1973.
231. Trudgill, P. *Accent, Dialect and the School.* London: Edward Arnold, 1975.
232. Verriour, P. "The Literary Language of Selected Four Year Old Children," unpublished doctoral dissertation, University of Alberta, 1979.
233. Vygotsky, L. *Mind in Society.* Cambridge, MA: Harvard University Press, 1978.
234. Vygotsky, L.S. Translated by Hanfmann and Vakar. *Thought and Language.* Cambridge, MA: MIT Press, 1962.
235. Walkerdine, W., and C. Sinha. "Developing Linguistic Strategies in Young Children," *Learning through Interaction.* New York: Teachers College Press, 1980.
236. Wardhaugh, Ronald. "Theories of Language Acquisition in Relation to Beginning Reading Instruction," *Reading Research Quarterly,* 7 (Fall 1971).
237. Weaver, C. *Psycholinguistics and Reading: From Process to Practice.* Cambridge, MA: Winthrop, 1980.
238. Weber, L. *The English Infant School and Informal Education.* Englewood Cliffs, NJ: Prentice-Hall, 1971.
239. Wells, G. *Learning through Interaction.* Cambridge, England: Cambridge University Press, 1980.
240. Wildman, D., and M. King. "Syntactic and Spatial Anticipation in Reading," *Reading Research Quarterly,* 14 (Winter 1979).
241. "Words in Color," *Current Approaches to Teaching Reading.* Washington, DC: NEA, 1968.
242. Yarger, S.J., and B.R. Joyce. "Going beyond the Data: Reconstructing Teacher Education," *Journal of Teacher Education,* 1977, 21-25.
243. Zutell, J. "Children's Spelling Strategies and Their Cognitive Development," in E. Henderson (Ed.), *Developmental and Cognitive Aspects of Learning to Spell.* Newark, DE: International Reading Association, 1980.

CHILDREN'S BOOKS AND POEMS

Asbjornsen, Peter C., and Jorgen E. Moe. *The Three Billy Goats Gruff.* Illustrated by Marcia Brown. New York: Harcourt Brace Jovanovich, 1976.

Baum, Frank L. *The Wizard of Oz.* New York: World, 1972.

Burningham, John. *The Blanket.* New York: Thomas Y. Crowell, 1976.

Burningham, John. *Come Away from the Water, Shirley.* New York: Thomas Y. Crowell, 1968.

Bruna, Dick. *B is for Bear.* London: Methuen Children's Books, 1967.

Carle, Eric. *The Very Hungry Caterpillar.* New York: Collins, 1979.

Carroll, Lewis. *Alice's Adventures in Wonderland.* New York: Macmillan, 1963.

Caudill, Rebecca. *A Pocketful of Cricket.* New York: Holt, Rinehart and Winston, 1964.

Crews, Donald. *Truck.* New York: Greenwillow, 1980.

Doakes, David. *My Book of Pretty Pussies* (unpublished version), 1980.

Einsel, Walter. *Did You Ever See?* New York: Scholastic, 1962.

Galdone, Paul. *The Three Bears (Goldilocks).* New York: Seabury Press, 1971.

Galdone, Paul. *The Three Billy Goats Gruff.* New York: Houghton Mifflin, 1973.

Ginsburg, M. *The Chick and the Duckling.* Illustrated by J.A. Arnego. London: Hamish Hamilton, 1977.

"Goldilocks and the Three Bears" ("The Story of the Three Bears") in *The Fairy Tale Treasury,* retold by Raymond Briggs. New York: Dell, 1972.

Hughes, Shirley. *Up and Up.* Englewood Cliffs, NJ: Prentice-Hall, 1979.

Hutchin, Pat. *Rosie's Walk.* New York: Macmillan, 1968.

Kent, Jack. *The Fat Cat: A Danish Folktale. Parents'.*

Kessler, Ethel, and Leonard Kessler. *Do Baby Bears Sit in Chairs?* New York: Doubleday & Coy, 1961.

Kraus, Robert. *Leo the Late Bloomer.* New York: Windmill, 1971.

Langstaff, John. *Over in the Meadow.* New York: Harcourt Brace Jovanovich, 1957.

Lionni, Leo. *Frederick.* New York: Pantheon, 1967.

Martin, Bill. *Brown Bear, Brown Bear, What Do You See?* New York: Holt, Rinehart and Winston, 1970.

Martin, Bill. *All Over Everything* (a poem). New York: Holt, Rinehart and Winston, 1973.

Martin, Bill. *Ten Little Squirrels.* New York: Holt, Rinehart and Winston, 1973.

Martin, Bill. *The Cock and Two Gold Coins.* New York: Holt, Rinehart and Winston, 1973.

McCracken, Robert A., and Marlene McCracken. *Reading Is Only the Tiger's Tail.* Los Angeles: Leswing Press, 1972.

McInnes, John. *The Ghost Said Boo.* Champaign, IL: Garrard, 1974.

McNaught, Harry. *Muppets in My Neighborhood.* New York: Random House, 1977.

Mayer, Mercer. *Battle of Bubble and Squeak.* New York: Parents' 1974.

Mayer, Mercer. *Just for You.* New York: Golden Press, 1975.

Ness, Evalene. *Sam, Bangs, and Moonshine.* New York: Holt, Rinehart and Winston, 1966.

Obligado, Lillian. *Three Little Kittens.* New York: Random House.

Paterson, Katherine. *The Road to Terabithia.* New York: Crowell, 1977.

Rojankovsky, Feodor. *The Tall Book of Mother Goose.* New York: Harper and Row, 1942.

Twain, Mark. *Adventures of Huckleberry Finn.* New York: Harper, 1884.

FREE AND INEXPENSIVE PAMPHLETS FOR PARENTS

"The Parents' Role in the Reading Process," *Parent Pages.* Redmond, WA: Child Care Informational Exchange, September-October, 1981.

Reading Begins at Home. New York: American Library Association and World Book-Childcraft International (nd).

How to Help Your Child Become a Better Writer. Urbana, IL: National Council of Teachers of English.

Good Books Make Reading Fun and *Summer Reading Is Important.* Newark, DE: International Reading Association (nd).

"Reading in the House." New York: Scholastic (nd).

References   179

IRA MICROMONOGRAPH SERIES*

How Can I Encourage My Primary Grade Child to Read? Molly Kayes Ransbury. 1972, 12 pp.

How Can I Get My Teenager to Read? Rosemary Winebrenner. 1971, 12 pp.

How Can I Help My Child Build Positive Attitudes toward Reading? Susan M. lel Glazer. 1980, 12 pp.

How Can I Help My Child Get Ready to Read? Norma Rogers. 1972, 24 pp.

How Can I Help My Child Learn to Read English as a Second Language? Marcia Baghban. 1972, 16 pp. (Also available in Spanish)

How Can I Prepare My Young Child for Reading? Paula C. Grinnell. 1984, 12 pp.

How Does My Child's Vision Affect His Reading? Donald W. Eberly. 1972, 12 pp.

What Books and Records Should I Get for My Preschooler? Norma Rogers. 1972, 20 pp.

What Is Reading Readiness? Norma Rogers. 1971, 16 pp.

Why Read Aloud to Children? Julie M.T. Chan. 1974, 12 pp.

*These booklets for parents may be purchased for $.35 each to IRA members and $.50 each to others (prepaid) by writing to the International Reading Association, P.O. Box 8139, Newark, Delaware 19714.

References